THE HERMENEUTIC OF DOGMA

AMERICAN ACADEMY OF RELIGION

DISSERTATION SERIES

Edited by

H. Ganse Little, Jr.

Number 11

THE HERMENEUTIC OF DOGMA

by

Thomas B. Ommen

———————————————————————

SCHOLARS PRESS
Missoula, Montana

THE HERMENEUTIC OF DOGMA

by

Thomas B. Ommen

Published by

SCHOLARS PRESS

for

The American Academy of Religion

Distributed by

SCHOLARS PRESS
University of Montana
Missoula, Montana   59801

THE HERMENEUTIC OF DOGMA

by

Thomas B. Ommen
Marquette University
Milwaukee, Wisconsin

Ph. D., 1973   Adviser:
Marquette University   Patrick J. Burns, S.J.

Library of Congress Cataloging in Publication Data

Ommen, Thomas B.
   The hermeneutic of dogma.

   (Dissertation series - American Academy of Reli-
gion ; no. 11)
   Originally presented as the author's thesis, Mar-
quette University, 1973.
   Bibliography: p.
   1. Theology--Methodology. 2. Hermeneutics.
3. Dogma. I. Title. II. Series: American
Academy of Religion. Dissertation series - American
Academy of Religion ; no. 11.
BR118.O49   1975   230   75-29493
ISBN 0-89130-039-2

Printed in the United States of America
1 2 3 4 5
Printing Department
University of Montana
Missoula, Montana   59801

TABLE OF CONTENTS

ABBREVIATIONS ix

INTRODUCTION xi

Chapter

I.   CATHOLICISM AND THE HERMENEUTIC PROBLEM . . . 1

Introduction: The Hermeneutic Problem
Catholicism and the Hermeneutic Problem:
     The Critique of Gerhard Ebeling
Tradition and Hermeneutic in Catholic Thought

II.   DOGMA AND THE HERMENEUTIC PROBLEM 61

Dogma and Historical Awareness
Changes in the Concept of Dogma
The Definition of Dogma by the Church
Dogma as "Revealed" Truth
The Hermeneutic of Dogma: Some Classical
     Approaches

III.   THE CONTEMPORARY HERMENEUTICAL DISCUSSION . . 105

Introduction
Historical Background: The Emerging Awareness
     of Historicality
The Philosophical Hermeneutic of Hans-Georg
     Gadamer
The New Hermeneutic
Summary and Critical Reflections

IV.   CONTEMPORARY HERMENEUTIC AND THE INTERPRETATION
      OF DOGMA 165

The Situation of Dogmatic Texts
The Situation of the Interpreter of Dogma

V.   THE TRUTH OF DOGMA 209

The Truth of Interpretation
The Hermeneutical Problem and the Truth of Dogma
The Hermeneutic of Dogma: Some Further
     Implications

BIBLIOGRAPHY 243

v

To Judith

ABBREVIATIONS

CIC	Codex Iuris Canonici.
DS	H. Denzinger and A. Schönmetzer, eds. Enchiridion Symbolorum, Definitionum et Declarationum de rebus fidei et morum. Freiburg: Herder, 1965.
EvT	Evangelische Theologie, Munich, 1934ff.
HthG	Handbuch theologischer Grundbegriffe, ed. by H. Fries. Munich, 1962.
Mansi	J. D. Mansi, ed. Sacrorum Conciliorum nova et amplissima collectio. Paris, 1899-1927.
MüThZ	Münchener Theologische Zeitschrift. Munich, 1950ff.
RAC	Reallexikon für Antike und Christentum, ed. by Th. Klausner. Stuttgart 1941 (1950) ff.
RGG	Die Religion in Geschichte und Gegenwart, ed. by K. Galling. 3rd edition. Tübingen, 1956-1962.
TT	Yves Congar. Tradition and Tradition in the Church. New York, 1966.
ThWNT	Theologisches Wörterbuch zum Neuen Testament, ed. by G. Kittel. Stuttgart, 1933ff.
WF	Gerhard Ebeling. Word and Faith. Philadelphia, 1963.
WGT	Gerhard Ebeling. Word of God and Tradition. Philadelphia, 1968.
WM	Hans-Georg Gadamer. Wahrheit und Methode. Grundzüge einer philosophischen Hermeneutik. Tübingen, 1965.

INTRODUCTION

The hermeneutical problem has emerged over the last
two centuries as a major topic of philosophical and theological interest. Reflection on hermeneutics is most
apparent in the German philosophical tradition extending
from Friedrich Schleiermacher and Wilhelm Dilthey in the
last century to the contemporary work of Martin Heidegger
and Hans-Georg Gadamer. This philosophical discussion has
been paralleled by a similar interest in German Protestant
theology, particularly in the Bultmannian school. In contrast to both of these movements, consideration of the
hermeneutical problem in Catholic theology is in an early
and tentative stage of development. This is particularly
evident in the scarcity of treatments of the hermeneutic of
dogma. Such a silence is especially surprising in light of
the crisis of meaning which seems to affect not only peripheral but central affirmations of faith as well in the modern
period. The purpose of this study is to contribute to a
developing Catholic discussion by formulating a hermeneutic
of dogma in light of contemporary German hermeneutics.

In the writing of this dissertation I received help
from many people. My gratitude goes, above all, to my direc-
tor, Fr. Patrick J. Burns, S.J., for his encouragement and
helpful suggestions. Thanks are also due to the other readers

xi

of the dissertation, Dr. Kenneth Hagen, Dr. W. Taylor
Stevenson, Fr. Tad Guzie, S.J., and Fr. Matthew Lamb.
For their help in preparation of the manuscript, I would
like to thank my wife, Judith, Dr. Mary Moscato, and the
skillful typist of the final text, Miss Camille Slowinski.

CHAPTER I

CATHOLICISM AND THE HERMENEUTIC PROBLEM

I. Introduction: The Hermeneutic Problem

Christianity is given the hermeneutical problem with
its bond to a historical revelation. The salvific events
of Christ's life at the heart of the Christian kerygma are
historical in origin, are recorded in a collection of historical documents, and are handed on in a tradition of
textual sources. The continuing responsibility of Christianity to reappropriate and reinterpret the sources of faith
is thus necessarily historical in character. The central
hermeneutical problem for Christianity is the need to interpret an authoritative textual tradition and to translate this
tradition into historical situations to which it no longer
directly speaks. Edward Schillebeeckx has succinctly summa-
rized the hermeneutical problem in this way:

> A serious tension is inherent in this situation. A
> message of God to men expressed and interpreted in
> a specific situation of the past becomes the norm
> for, and the test of our Christian faith today--a
> faith that is experienced in a totally different
> historical situation. The essential implication of
> this is that we can comprehend this biblical word
> in faith and only through a reinterpretative under-
> standing of the faith and in no other way.[1]

---

[1]Edward Schillebeeckx, "Towards a Catholic use of Hermeneutics," in God the Future of Man (New York: Sheed and
Ward, 1968), p. 6.

The explicit reflection upon this process of "reinterpretive understanding" is the task of Christian hermeneutics.

The hermeneutical problem has been with Christianity throughout its history, emerging as a topic of special interest particularly at those points when interpretation of Scripture and tradition was blocked for one reason or another. It is only in the modern period, however, that the full historical dimensions of hermeneutic have become apparent. Despite stirrings of historical consciousness in ancient Greece and in later Western tradition, the real emergence of historical awareness is in the seventeenth and eighteenth centuries.[2] By the end of the nineteenth century, as Ernst Troeltsch recognized, the problem of faith and history had replaced the question of faith and science as the central concern of Christianity.

Historical consciousness brought with it a clearer appreciation of the time-difference that separates the Christian Church from its biblical origins and from the monuments of tradition. From a historical perspective, the complexity and difficulty of interpreting a biblical or a conciliar text became apparent for the first time. Critical historical awareness made it possible to see the Christian past clearly as past, but it also seemed to undermine the living continuity of past and present upon which Christianity depends.

---

[2]For a sketch of this development, see Gerhard Krüger, "Die Geschichte im Denken der Gegenwart," in Freiheit und Weltverwaltung (Freiburg-Munich: K. Alber, 1958), p. 102.

Critical historical awareness is, in a real sense, antitheti-
cal to tradition. The past properly becomes tradition only
when its claim on the present is recognized, when it is
shown to be significant, and in this way is handed on. The
conflict which preoccupied dialectical theology between
positivism and historicism on the one hand and "faith" or
"existential" interpretation on the other is essentially a
conflict between the past viewed from the standpoint of critical historical method and the past existentially perceived.
The new quest for the historical Jesus, the debate between
the schools of Pannenberg and Bultmann, and the resurrection
of modern variants of nineteenth century liberal theology--
all reveal how far the tension is from any final resolution.

Coupled to the awareness of the "pastness" of the authoritative texts of faith and the hermeneutical difficulties
this awareness poses has been a clearer recognition of their
relativity. The immersion of Christian tradition in history
has subjected it to the contingency and limitations of its
historical forms. How is such historicality to be harmonized
with the Christian claim to "absolute" truth? The modern
wariness of any dogmatic claims to truth has been felt by
Christianity as a challenge to the truth of its own tradition. The dilemma of modern man is how to think historically
without retreating to total relativism. A major concern in
the contemporary hermeneutical discussion has been to combine
the demands of critical historical method and the historical
relativity it seems to entail with a recognition of the

existentially perceived truth of the tradition for Christianity.

The theological hermeneutical discussion of the present day is marked by two apparent characteristics. In the first place, it has been almost exclusively a preoccupation of Protestant theologians. As Gerhard Ebeling has pointed out, "the subject Word of God and hermeneutics combines two concepts which are perhaps more representative than any others of the approach that has determined theological thinking in the last four decades, and that still determines it today and must determine it in the train of the Reformation."[3] The centrality of the hermeneutical problem is nowhere more apparent than in Bultmannian theology, the school that Ebeling represents, and it is this discussion that will be a primary focus throughout this study. In light of the importance ascribed to the question of hermeneutics in Protestant theology, it is surprising to discover that the topic has prompted comparatively little interest among Roman Catholics. Eberhard Simons has noted with amazement, for example, the inadequacy of the treatment of hermeneutic in the basic Catholic theological reference works. Such articles are usually limited to a few general remarks about rules for interpreting biblical texts or a historical sketch of the

---

[3] WF, 305. The main themes and scope of this hermeneutical discussion will be presented in detail in Chapter III of this study.

"four senses" theory which has characterized the Catholic approach to biblical interpretation up to the present day.[4] Catholic interest in hermeneutics has generally remained at a level of investigation long since left behind in the philosophical and Protestant discussions. Hermeneutic is viewed strictly as an auxiliary discipline to biblical exegesis dealing with the theory of and rules for interpreting biblical texts. More fundamental questions of a philosophical or ontological nature are most often not treated.[5] In recent years, Catholic contributions to the hermeneutical discussion have begun to appear, but such a discussion remains in a very early stage of development.[6]

---

[4]Eberhard Simons, "Die Bedeutung der Hermeneutik für die katholische Theologie," *Catholica* 21 (1967), 184. For similar criticisms of the inadequacy of the Catholic hermeneutical discussions see Albert Keller, "Hermeneutik und christlicher Glaube," *Theologie und Philosophie* 44 (1969), 25. For an example of the cursory treatment of hermeneutic in Catholic theological lexikons see "Hermeneutik," *LTK*, 3rd ed., II, 435ff.

[5]R. Lapointe, *Les trois dimensions de l'herméneutique* (Paris: J. Gabalda et Cie, 1967), pp. 14-15 notes a gap between Catholics and Protestants in a willingness to seek a total hermeneutical perspective grounded in philosophy.

[6]Günter Stachel, *Die neue Hermeneutik: Ein Überblick* (Munich: Kösel, 1967), pp. 61ff. dates the beginning of Catholic hermeneutical concern in the years after Vatican II, particularly in a number of articles written by German exegetes. See, e.g., Rudolf Schnackenburg, "Zur Auslegung der Schrift in unserer Zeit," *Bibel und Leben* 4 (1964), 220-236. More recent contributions include the aforementioned articles by Simons and Keller (footnote #4) as well as Simons' full length study *Theologisches Verstehen* (co-authored by Konrad Hecker) (Düsseldorf: Patmos, 1969); E. Schillebeeckx, "Towards a Catholic use of Hermeneutics," in *God the Future of Man*, op. cit.; Oswald Loretz and W. Strolz, eds., *Die hermeneutische Frage in der Theologie* (Freiburg: Herder, 1968); Emerich Coreth, *Grundfragen der Hermeneutik* (Freiburg: Herder,

Apart from its Protestant character, a second apparent characteristic of the contemporary theological discussion of hermeneutics is its concentration on problems of biblical interpretation. This is not to say that hermeneutics has remained in its classical role as a subdivision within biblical studies dealing with the theory of text interpretation. Rather, the hermeneutical task, particularly as seen by the theologians in the Bultmannian school, "embraces the whole theological enterprise as a movement of language, from the Word of God attested in Scripture to the preached sermon in which God speaks anew."[7] This movement from text to proclamation involves theology necessarily in ontological questions. What are the universal structures of understanding and of reality as a whole which make this movement from text to proclamation possible? This broader philosophical concern has prompted a continuing dialogue between theologians and philosophers grappling with the hermeneutical problem. What has been lacking in both Protestant theology and in the few Catholic contributions that have appeared, however, is a systematic application of these broader dimensions of hermeneutical theory to problems of interpreting doctrinal as well as scriptural texts. Such an investigation is of particular

---

1969); and René Marlé Introduction to Hermeneutics (New York: Herder, 1967).

[7]James M. Robinson, "Introduction," in The New Hermeneutic. New Frontiers in Theology, vol. II (New York: Harper and Row, 1964), pp. 3-4.

interest to Catholic theology because of its strong affirmation of a non-scriptural textual tradition. Albert Keller
has noted, for example, that although the problematic of
interpreting magisterial statements is particularly crucial
at this point in Catholic history, there are very few works
which actually seek such a hermeneutical foundation for
dogmatic interpretation.[8]

What explains this lack of a Catholic discussion of
theological hermeneutic in general and of the hermeneutic of
dogma in particular? This question is not raised arbitrarily.
The history of the post-Reformation Catholic Church demon-
strates, to a large extent, a continuing opposition to emerging historical consciousness and methodology. This apparent
gap between Catholic theology and the intellectual currents
which have molded the contemporary hermeneutical discussion
at least raises the possibility that there is an intrinsic
gap between the Catholic understanding of faith and tradition
and an adequate hermeneutical theory. Such an opinion has
been stated most forcefully by the evangelical theologian,
Gerhard Ebeling. Ebeling contends that there is no hermeneutical problem for the Catholic Church; the Catholic view of
tradition is an "answer" to the hermeneutical problem.

---

[8]Albert Keller, "Hermeneutik und christlicher Glaube,"
p. 25. One of the few exceptions to this silence is the
article by Piet Schoonenberg as well as others in the same
issue of Tijdschrift voor Theologie 8 (1968), 243-347 published under the title "De Interpretatie van het dogma." All
of the articles were translated into German and published as
Die Interpretation des Dogmas (Düsseldorf: Patmos, 1969).
References will be to the German version.

Ebeling's elaboration and justification of this contention
will be discussed in some detail for three reasons: 1) As
one of the main figures in the "New Hermeneutic" he has contributed some of the clearest and most comprehensive reflections on the problem of hermeneutics. His demarcation of
his own developed hermeneutical position from that of Catholic thought therefore provides a clear avenue to some of the
key hermeneutical issues facing Catholic theology; 2) While
Ebeling's own hermeneutic has by no means found general
acceptance in Protestant theology, his criticism of the
Catholic "solution" to the hermeneutical problem is representative of a general Protestant attitude. A careful look
at his critique is thus quite helpful in clarifying both
the points of contact as well as the points of difference
between Protestant and Catholic approaches to the hermeneutical problem; 3) Catholic dogma and the mode of its interpretation are for Ebeling the key illustration of the
Catholic "flight" from the hermeneutical problem. A study
of his critique of Catholic dogma and of his own counter-
position on the interpretation of dogmatic statements thus
points to the specific problem of this investigation--the
elaboration of a Catholic hermeneutic of dogma in light of
the philosophical and Protestant hermeneutical discussions.

II. Catholicism and the Hermeneutic Problem

The Critique of Gerhard Ebeling

The basis for the hermeneutical problem is for Ebeling
the continuing need of Christianity to "actualize" a

historically given revelation. When the historicity of revelation is preserved, its givenness in a past textual tradition, the hermeneutical problem asserts itself. In the
history of Christian thought, however, Ebeling finds three
possible ways of actualizing revelation which undermine or
evade the historicity of revelation and the hermeneutical
problem. One of these possibilities is the identification
of the written Scriptural text with revelation. Literalism
and fundamentalism fall into this category; there is no real
hermeneutical problem for the fundamentalist because the
letter of Scripture is infallibly certain and clear. Problems of faith are solved by a simple dogmatization of the
doctrinal and moral teaching of Scripture. What is overlooked is the historical context of the original teaching
and the impossibility of simply leaping over the gap between
the text and present: "Specific instructions of Jesus to his
disciples are not susceptible of direct and general realization in the present."[9]

A second possibility is the "enthusiastic" or "contemplative" actualization of revelation. From the contemplative
perspective, the believer and God stand in a direct, mystical interaction to the exclusion of the past events of revelation. The hermeneutical problem of the "horizontal,"
historical separation of the Church from its origins is

_____

[9]Ebeling elaborates the three alternatives in WF, 32-35;
cf. WGT, 20ff.

dissolved in a "vertical" relationship to God. The consequence is a "spiritualizing severance of the correlation
between the Church and the historicity of the revelation in
Jesus Christ."[10] The contemplative outlook involves the
critical dissolution of a concept of the Church. Because
God and individual stand in direct interaction, the need
for community is removed; the Church, if it is affirmed at
all, is always an invisible reality, not identifiable with
any visible, historical community.

The third type of actualization which evades the hermeneutical problem is the Catholic approach, which Ebeling
labels "realistic metaphysical actualization."[11] In Catholicism, the historical revelation is mediated through a
variety of material forms, e.g., through sacraments. The
encounter with revelation is lifted out of a framework of
the interpretation of historical texts and thus escapes the
hermeneutical problem. Revelation is so identified with a
visible present reality, that the scandal of its "pastness"
and thus its proper historicity is removed. The Church,
above all, stands in Catholicism as the present actualization
of the revelation event. The Church is the "mystical body of
Christ"--the present medium of revelation--which "swallows
up" the past events, the "perfect tense" of revelation.[12]

---

[10]WGT, 23-24.

[11]WF, 34ff.

[12]WF, 35.

The relationship of Scripture and tradition throughout the history of the Catholic Church is for Ebeling the primary illustration of the Catholic destruction of the hermeneutical problem. "Realistic metaphysical actualization" in its ecclesiastical form carries implications for the interpretation of Scripture which became apparent in the early Catholic period of biblical interpretation and which have molded the Catholic approach to Scripture down to the present day. For the early Fathers, especially Tertullian and Irenaeus, the normative meaning of revelation was that which was original and apostolic. But because no clear and unambiguous original historical meaning could be ascertained, the process of tradition, guaranteed by apostolic succession, was given normative significance.[13] This location of authority in a fixed rule of faith and in individual interpreters necessitated a de-emphasis of revelation as past event. Revelation in effect was "dehistoricized" and this dehistoricization persisted into the Middle Ages and finally into the modern day. As evidence of this Process, Ebeling points to the "sterility" of historical writing and methodology in the patristic period and in the Middle Ages.

> What is the explanation...of the sterility of histor-
> ical writing of early and medieval Christianity? It
> lies in the fact that the living apprehension of the
> historical revelation had been transformed from an
> historical activity into a thing, a mere state of
> affairs. The reality of Christ had been transformed

---

[13]Ebeling, The Problem of Historicity in the Church and Its Proclamation, (Philadelphia: Fortress, 1967), p. 56.

12

into a sacramental event; relics had taken the
place of the reality of past history; the living
interpretation of the Scriptures had been replaced
by an apostolically guaranteed tradition; the vital
eschatological dualism of the civitas dei and the
civitas terrena had become the visible juxtaposi-
tion of Church and not-Church, replacing faith
based on history by immediate experience; the
critical search for historical truth had been replaced by a simple acceptance of tradition; the
vision of the dialectical multiplicity of phenomena had been replaced by a schematized and mythological view of a wholly black and white universe.
World history had lost all interest because the
Church had finally filled the horizon. Church
History was essentially uninteresting because in
its contemporary form its whole past had become
contemporary.[14]

The possibility of a tension between the Scriptures and oral

tradition was not recognized by Scholastic theology. An

uncritical, nonhistorical relationship was instead assumed,

to the extent that the terms sacra scriptura, sacra pagina,

and theologia could be used almost interchangably.[15]

This same basic understanding of the relationship of

Scripture and tradition was clearly sanctioned, Ebeling

believes, at the first Vatican Council. The developing auth-

ority of the magisterium, given the mark of infallibility at

Vatican I, represents the final triumph of the authority of

the present over the past. By attributing final authority

in interpretation to the official magisterium, the possibility

of criticism by Scripture is removed: "Thus the Church is

protected from the outset against the possibility that a

---

[14]WGT, 20-21.

[15]WGT, 103.

criticism might be raised on the basis of the Scriptures. The Church itself stands as iudex above the Scriptures."[16] The argument over "two sources" versus "one source" of revelation has little relevance as long as the magisterium is the final court of appeal in determining what is revelation. The free critical voice of the Scriptures has been effectively silenced; there is no possibility in Catholicism of the traditum being adequately distinguished from the actus tradendi. Both have blended together in the form of the continuing presence of the Church, and the hermeneutical problem, in effect, has been solved.

> In the formula "Scripture and Tradition" is comprised the Catholic response to the hermeneutic problem of theology. The revelation to which Scripture bears witness cannot be rightly understood apart from the Tradition represented in the Church. Indeed the Church as the Tradition is the authoritative interpretation of the revelation to which Scripture bears witness.[17]

The Church, by thus elevating itself over the historical givenness of Scripture, "escapes from hermeneutic responsibility, whatever freedom of activity it may still retain."[18]

The Catholic notion of dogma provides the clearest example of the Catholic evasion of "hermeneutic responsibility." Dogma combines an assertion of a guaranteed relationship to revelation with the jurisdictional power of the magisterium. The hermeneutical problem--how to reach the

---

[16]Ebeling, The Problem of Historicity, 56.

[17]WGT, 126.

[18]WGT, 134; cf. WF, 305.

meaning of revelation in its historical form and translate
this meaning into the present situation of faith--is solved
by purely formal means. The claim to the truth of revelation is "bracketed together" with the claim to formal absolute authority. Nowhere is it more apparent that there is
for Catholicism no real hermeneutical problem, for the
revelational truth of dogma is ascertained finally not by
the adequacy of interpretation, but purely by the jurisdictional authority of the magisterium. "The question as to
which interpretation is correct not only can but must be
decided jurisdictionally, and the decision possesses the
authority of the canon itself."[19] The "authority" over
faith is finally not that of a textual tradition but of a
court of law. A new and separate action of the Holy Spirit
is asserted apart from that involved in Scripture itself.
Rather than providing an ecclesiological witness to or confession of the revealed truth of Scripture, dogma adds to
the act of revelation in Christ a second, independently produced source of revelation. The correlation between the
definitions of the Church and the original sources of revelation is decided not hermeneutically but authoritatively by
an infallible legal power. There is in Catholicism an a
priori impossibility of any contradiction between dogma and
Scripture. "The Church can only grow, its doctrine can only

---

[19]Ebeling, The Problem of Historicity, 88-89; cf.
WF, 38-39.

develop, by making inviolate its identity and continuity.
Any change it undergoes is a purely biological one, there is
no real historical development."[20] This biological continuity is the only explanation, as Ebeling sees it, for the
mariological definitions of the last two centuries; the
definitions of the Immaculate Conception and Assumption completely sundered history and revelation and elevated ecclesiastical positivism above theological science.[21] The
necessary consequence of this arbitrary relationship to
history and to the hermeneutical problem is a vulnerability
of Catholicism in the face of historical criticism. In the
last few centuries, the historical claims of the Church, for
example those regarding its own origins, have been particularly subjected to historical criticism. In the face of its
hermeneutical inadequacies, the response of Catholicism has
most often been dogmatic and apologetic rather than historical. Conflicts between history and faith have been settled
by an appeal to authority rather than by an appeal to evidence.[22]

The intrinsic unsoundness of Catholic hermeneutic becomes even more apparent when juxtaposed to the outlook of
the Reformers. The Reformers' critique of Catholicism carries
profound hermeneutical implications both for the interpreta-

---

[20]WGT, 23.

[21]Ebeling, The Problem of Historicity, 57.

[22]WGT, 19; cf. p. 23.

tion of Scripture as well as for the interpretation of doctrine. In the first place, the Scripture principle of the
Reformers removed the need for a source of authoritative
interpretation alongside the Scriptural text. Scripture
for the Reformers possessed its own principle of interpreta-
tion--a claritas which obviated the need for a traditional
guide to authentic interpretation.[23] Although Luther recognized the occasional obscurity of the "letter," the "spiritual" res or subject matter of Scripture enjoyed a clarity
which guaranteed its understandability and salvific efficacy.[24] This res or center of Old and New Testaments was
identified by Luther with the justifying word encountered in
Christ. The justification principle, particularly in Pauline
terms, became the formal principle for critique not only of
tradition, but of Scripture itself. Thus Hebrews and James,
to the extent that they gave inadequate expression to Christ,
were given secondary canonical status by Luther.

The clear separation of the "letter" and "spirit" of
Scripture gave Protestantism an openness to the hermeneutical
problem. Because the written text was not automatically identified with the Word of God, its historicity or pastness
could be taken seriously. Luther placed an emphasis on the

----

[23]WF, 306. cf. Ebeling, "Hermeneutik," RGG, 3rd. ed.,
III, 251.

[24]For a thorough presentation of Luther's doctrine of
claritas scripturae see F. Beisser, Claritas Scripturae bei
Martin Luther (Göttingen: Vandenhoeck and Ruprecht, 1966).

literal sense of Scripture, and after 1517 clearly departed
from the fourfold sense schema of medieval interpretation.[25]
A humanistic concern with the original languages of Scripture, especially Hebrew, and with the desirability and
necessity of translations into living tongues also accompanied Luther's preoccupation with the scriptural text.[26] The
historical meaning or "letter" of the text was never identified, however, with the Gospel; the written word remained
"law" until it was translated into proclamation.[27] The movement of meaning or "word-event," in Ebeling's terms, was from
the situation of the text in its historical pastness into the
changing concrete situation of faith in the present. This
means that for Protestantism as for Luther the Gospel is the
fruit of a constantly renewed act of interpretation; Christianity by necessity is given a hermeneutical responsibility.[28]
No single "meaning" of Scripture or content of revelation can
be isolated from the multitude of "traditions" in which the

---

[25]"Hermeneutik," RGG, 3rd ed., III, 251.

[26]Ibid.

[27]Ebeling, The Problem of Historicity, 14. "The word of
Scripture, considered as a written word and therefore as a
word belonging to the past, is not the Word of God; in this
form it would always be only Law and not Gospel. Instead the
word of Scripture is the Word of God when it is a word proclaimed in the present, a viva vox evangelii--naturally, in
the form of interpretation based on the word of Scripture, and
yet in such a way that this word confronts us not as something
written but as an oral word, that is, one which is uttered
here and now."

[28]WGT, 26; cf. "Luther: II-Theologie," RGG, 3rd ed.,
IV, 506, and The Problem of Historicity, 14-15.

one "tradition" of Christianity is handed on. The center of
Scripture and of Christian tradition as a whole is not a
static system of doctrinal truths, but the event of living
proclamation.

> The substance of tradition is not simply a doctrine,
> nor is it simply the report of an historical event.
> In the strict sense it is the eschatological act of
> God in Jesus Christ. Of course it is handed down
> as witness to a specific event in history and con-
> sequently is based upon the original testimony to
> this event. But this act forms the content of tra-
> dition not as a historical event but as an event
> which is proclaimed and present. Moreover, this
> tradition is transmitted not by recitation of the
> testimony of the first witnesses but by a proclama-
> tion which results from this testimony. By its
> very nature, then, the substance of tradition can-
> not be absolutely determined. All that can be
> determined at any given time is the witness to it,
> which now continues in its own right to form tra-
> dition.[29]

This understanding of tradition preserves a distinction between the one "tradition" of Christianity--the "word-event"
of Christ himself--and the multiplicity of "traditions" in
which this event is witnessed and handed on. In the first
place, a distinction is preserved between the manifold "traditions" within Scripture itself and the "center" of Scripture which is the saving event of Christ. The unity of
Scripture cannot be encapsulated in a timeless doctrinal
system nor in the form of a particular doctrine or group of
writings within Scripture--a "canon within the canon."[30]

---

[29]Ebeling, The Problem of Historicity, 84-85.

[30]WGT, 144.

Secondly, a distinction is preserved between the text of
Scripture and particular interpretations, whether those of
the Church as a whole, e.g. in doctrines, or of individuals.
Interpretation is never over and done with; the Scripture is
remembered and handed on only by the continuing act of interpretation in the changing historical situation of faith. The
Church cannot be identified with the Word of God, but stands
under it, speaking "authoritatively" only to the extent that
its witness brings the Gospel to expression in any given
historical situation.[31] The essence of Christian tradition
in all its forms, scriptural and post-scriptural, is the transmission and bringing to expression of the word-event of Christ
and not a Christian form of the Law.

The principles of sola scriptura and sola fide provide
Protestantism, in contrast to Catholicism, with the capability and responsibility of coming to terms with the hermeneutical problem. No more important evidence of the difference
which Ebeling sees between the Protestant and Catholic approaches to the hermeneutical problem exists than the different ways
of actualizing revelation: "the antithesis between Catholicism
and Protestantism rests on the different understanding of the
historical ἄπαξ (once-for-allness) of revelation." The sola
fide principle of the Reformation expresses the conviction
that revelation comes only through the ever-renewed Word of
God, and that any definitive or "infallible" human interpreta-

---

[31]WGT, 136.

tions of the Word of God correspond only to Law.

> The sola fide of the Reformation doctrine of justifi-
> cation contains both a rejection of any existing ways
> of ensuring present actualization of revelation,
> whether ontological, sacramental or hierarchical, and
> also positively includes an understanding of actuali-
> zation in the sense of genuinely historic, personal
> encounter...the sola fide destroys all secretly docetic
> views of revelation which evade the historicalness of
> revelation by making it a history sui generis, a
> sacred area from which the critical historical method
> must be anxiously debarred. In the Reformers' view,
> both revelation and faith are discovered in their
> genuine historicalness, and that quite definitely
> means that faith is exposed to all the vulnerability
> and ambiguity of the historical.[32]

Relics, saints, dogma, a visible "sacred" or "salvation" his-

tory--all these are "secularized" in the Protestant outlook.

The Catholic understanding of history, in which the Word is

bound in fixed, definable historical categories is thus "de-

mythologized."[33] Catholicism faces a persistent vulnerabil-

ity in the face of historical criticism. In contrast, the

breakdown of the mythology of the distinction between

"sacred" and "profane" history opens Protestantism to a com-

plete acceptance of critical historical methodology. It per-

mits Scripture to be fully critical of tradition as well as

permitting criticism of the letter of Scripture with the

criterion of Christ. No element of tradition or passage of

Scripture is automatically revelation. Dogmatic presupposi-

tions can stand neither over exegesis nor over Church History.

This immersion of tradition in history is an extension of the

---

[32]WF, 56.

[33]WGT, 17-18.

Christian understanding of the Incarnation. God is present
in history not in a miraculous, visible interruption of the
historical continuum, but, paradoxically, in weakness and
suffering, "behind" the ordinary events of history. The God
of the Bible is not the omnipotent, working hypothesis God,
but one of impotence and weakness who allows himself to be
forced out of the world and onto the Cross. The Protestant
recognition that the appropriate form of theology is a theologia crucis and not a theologia gloriae is for Ebeling the
ultimate explanation for the bond of Protestant theology to
history and to the hermeneutical problem.[34]

Ebeling recognizes that this somewhat idealized sketch
of the Protestant compatibility with the hermeneutical problem
does not fit all of the facts of Protestant church history.
After the Reformation, Protestant Orthodoxy soon lost sight of
the fundamental hermeneutical insights of the Reformers. Subjected to Catholic criticism and in the face of internal
divisions, Protestant Orthodoxy sought new guarantees for the
clarity of Scripture. The result was a doctrine of verbal
inspiration which guaranteed the text of Scripture and a clear
literal sense right down to the pointing of the Hebrew letter-
ing. By providing a foundation for an infallibly true literal
sense of Scripture, Protestant Orthodoxy supplied, in effect,
a modified tradition principle. The "letter" of Scripture
was identified with the Word of God, and Luther's distinction

---

[34]WF, 154-155.

of letter and spirit and desire to assure the critical freedom of Gospel over tradition and dogmatics were lost.[35]
Ebeling recognizes that it was in part a lack of clarity on
the hermeneutic problem in the Reformation that led to this
turn of events. Luther had underestimated the lack of clarity
that can affect the scriptural text.[36] The simplistic doctrine of sola scriptura employed by Orthodoxy to solve the
hermeneutical problem was seriously challenged by the emergence of historical criticism in the seventeenth and eighteenth centuries. The response of Orthodoxy to the challenge,
just as in Catholicism, was the separation of historical and
dogmatic methods. The task of Protestant theology today, as
Ebeling sees it, is to harmonize the Reformers' insight into
the nature of Scripture and faith with critical historical
methodology.[37] Ebeling's own approach to theology is an indication of this new demand placed on theology in the contemporary age. The two main foci of his method are, on the one
hand, a recovery of the legitimate insights of Reformation
thought and, on the other, an attention to the modern experience of reality, particularly the modern understanding of
history and critical historical method.[38]

Just as Protestant Orthodoxy inadequately separated the

[35]"Hermeneutic," RGG, 3rd ed., III, 252.

[36]WF, 308.

[37]WGT, 107.

[38]WF, 9, 18.

letter and spirit of Scripture, it also identified doctrine
with the Word of God. Luther had by no means proclaimed a
"dogmaless" Christianity. Doctrine, particularly the teaching of the first four Councils, was embraced in the Reformation as a legitimate element in the Christian message.
Luther's focus, however, was on the proclamative dimension
of Church teaching. Doctrina Christiana was authentic to the
extent that it preserved the living power of the Gospel; dogma
was clearly subservient to the normative Word of God. "It is
always a question of the doctrina Christiana, the doctrine
that accords with the Word of God, in which nothing else but
the Word of God itself comes to expression."[39] "Pure" doc-
trine--that which reflected the Word of God--was, however,
absolutely binding for Luther even though its authority rested
in the Word.[40] Ebeling believes that this presupposition
made ambiguous the distinction of Church teaching and Word of
God, and that the consequences of this ambiguity became apparent in Protestant Orthodoxy. Already in the writings of
Melancthon, there is a tendency to equate the Gospel with a
given body of Church teachings. Just as the task of contemporary Protestant theology is to seek a more adequate way of
distinguishing the letter and spirit of Scripture, it also has
the task of redefining the notion of Church teaching: "What
separates us today from the age of the Reformation and from

---

[39]WF, 76-77.

[40]Ibid.

24

the age of Orthodoxy, is, that we must go much farther than they did in distinguishing between Word of God, holy scripture, proclamation, doctrine, and theology."[41]   The advantage Protestantism possesses over Catholicism is that its own tradition makes such a distinction both possible and necessary.

While Protestant Orthodoxy and, to a certain extent, the Reformers tended to "blur the distinction" between Word of God and Church doctrine, Ebeling seeks to distinguish more carefully each from the other. If defined in a broad sense, doctrine can include all forms of Church witness in as much as all have a content or meaning.[42]   More narrowly defined, however, doctrine is Church teaching, and still more narrowly and accurately distinguished from other forms of Church witness, it is "the limited concentration of that witness in regulative statements which are generally accepted in the Church."[43]   In this carefully delimited sense, doctrine is not the only or even the primary way in which the Word of God comes to expression. Indeed, because of his emphasis on the proclamative character of the Word of God, Ebeling deemphasizes the function of doctrine as an expression of the Christian Gospel. Doctrine tends toward the abstract and universal;

---

[41]WF, 174-175. cf. WGT, 168-169.

[42]WGT, 169.

[43]Ibid.

Word of God in the proper sense tends toward oral communication and interpersonal encounter.[44]

Although Ebeling's definition of Church doctrine includes an assertion of its "regulative" character, the "regulative" force of doctrine in an authentically Protestant perspective is far removed from the Catholic understanding. The authority of Church teaching is not guaranteed by any formal marks it might possess, but by its power to bring to expression the Word of God. Luther was willing to speak of the "infallibility" of the universal Church, but this authority was not concentrated in any judge or representative of the Church as a whole.[45] No institutional teaching authority could decide absolutely the revealed truth of any scriptural passage or Church teaching. The Protestant Scripture principle emerged, in fact, in the dispute over doctrinal authority. It involved two basic questions: 1) What are the authoritative sources of Church doctrine? 2) What is the ultimate source of authority in disputed questions?

> The reason the question of doctrinal authority divides
> itself into these two subordinate questions is that
> the authoritative sources of church doctrine do not
> allow a direct and obvious determination of what church
> doctrine is. These sources also must be interpreted.
> And wherever the task of interpretation is involved,
> the possibility of differences of opinion arises, so
> that the question must be posed as to which interpre-
> tation is correct. In a curious way, therefore, the
> problem of interpretation coalesces with the problem

---

[44]WGT, 169-170.

[45]Ebeling, The Problem of Historicity, 90.

> of law, and the hermeneutical problem fuses with
> the jurisdictional problem. On closer view, of
> course, this coalescence of the two is absurd,
> since the correctness of interpretation can be
> proven only by way of interpretation itself. If
> an interpretation cannot create its own authority,
> no authority can be created for it by the introduc-
> tion of another, formal or legal authority, for
> such an action would upset the very authority which
> interpretation lays claim to, namely, the authority
> of the reality (Sache) being discussed.[46]

Once again, the incompatibility of any notion of formal
authority and hermeneutical responsibility is stressed. Continuity of the Church with its origins and its visible unity
are products of the adequacy of individual acts of interpretation.

Ebeling refuses to recognize an avenue out of the hermeneutical problem of doctrine in the distinction of "content"
and "form." The authority of doctrine is not preserved by
pointing to the essential unchanging "content" of a teaching
while admitting the time-conditioned and possibly ambiguous
or even incorrect "form" in which it is presented: "For how
can the content of a proposition be taken seriously without
taking its wording seriously."[47] Nor can "unchanging" or
"absolute" Church doctrine be adequately distinguished from
the arbitrary opinions of individual theologians.[48] Doctrine
attains meaning or content only by the path of interpretation.
The truth of interpretation can only be judged by its adequacy and convincing character and not by its formal authority.

---

[46]Ebeling, The Problem of Historicity, 87-88.

[47]WF, 178.

[48]WGT, 162-163.

Doctrine is not automatically binding; it is binding only when reinterpreted and reappropriated meaningfully in the changing context of faith. Tradition is not something that mechanically endures from one generation to another. Unlike biological or natural continuity, the hallmark of the continuity of human history is the _historicity_ of men. Responsibility, appropriation, repetition are all involved in man's remembrance of the past. Tradition, including doctrinal tradition, really only exists when men freely consent to it and make it their own.

> The foundation of historical continuity rests not on something that automatically endures from the past into the present but instead on what is spoken, heard and received from the past within the present. From this point of view alone can we speak of tradition.[49]

Because of this focus on free remembrance and handing on of doctrinal tradition, Ebeling places the final "court of appeal" in interpreting the meaning of doctrine in the conscience of the individual Christian. The individual must consent to doctrine in a free responsible act, and this cannot be forced upon him by external authority. Just as in the interpretation of Scripture, agreement or continuity with the past is founded finally in the adequacy of interpretation and thus in the agreement of text and exposition:

> Yet how can this be tested? Solely by participating in the theological task of identifying Church doctrine. We are confronted here, precisely as with holy scripture, by the hermeneutic problem. The

---

[49]Ebeling, _The Problem of Historicity_, 38-39. cf. "Tradition," _RGG_, 3rd ed., VI, 976-984, and _WF_, 178-179.

> agreement between text and exposition can be
> determined only by means of the exposition it-
> self. Demonstrating and testing agreement with
> the teaching of the confessions is possible
> only by means of theological study. Identity
> with the doctrine of the church can be estab-
> lished only in the process of identifying the
> church's doctrine.[50]

An individual may be said to understand doctrine only when

he appropriates it existentially and reexpresses it in his

own terms.

The elevation of individual conscience to the level of

the "final court of appeal" in interpretation of doctrine

also entails, in Ebeling's opinion, a recognition of the

possibility of criticism. Doctrine must be examined in

light of the subject matter of faith to which it witnesses.

Its authority rests finally on its connection to the Word of

God. Harmony with Scripture and its power to "set preach-

ing free" are the marks of true doctrine.[51] Just as individ-

ual passages and even books within Scripture do not automati-

cally qualify as Word of God by their place in the canon, so

doctrine enjoys no formal mark that makes it revelation.

Both Scripture and doctrine must be criticized in light of

the subject-matter which they express and thus in light of

the eschatological event of Christ.[52] Criticism may extend

---

[50]WF, 178.

[51]WGT, 179.

[52]A question that remains to be explored is the origin
of the principle of Sachkritik. Is it the "center" of Scripture, as Ebeling maintains, or a product of the interpreter's
preunderstanding?

to the point where doctrinal formulae lose their soteriological effectiveness and as a consequence are left behind
in the passage of Church history.

The location of final authority of interpretation in
individual conscience and the exposure of Scripture and
tradition to criticism and possible rejection raise the
question, Ebeling recognizes, of the unity of the Church.
Despite his focus on the individual believer, Ebeling is not
unaware of the importance of community to Christian faith.
The "homological" structure of faith--the consent and testimony to belief--is initially an individual act. Faith involves the identification of an individual with the liberat-
ing Word outside himself which summons him to believe. This
identification of an individual with proclamation leads him
necessarily, however, to testimony--to a summons to others
to believe as well. This unanimity with other believers "is
a not unimportant but necessarily secondary 'moment' in the
structure of faith."[53] Communal testimony to belief in the
form of Church doctrine is a necessary part of faith, but
"there can be no doctrinal decision whose correctness can
be formally proven and therefore there can be no unity of
the church founded upon formal law."[54] Ebeling maintains
that there never has been a universal visibly united Church;

---

[53]Ebeling, Theology and Proclamation: Dialogue with
Bultmann (Philadelphia: Fortress, 1966), pp. 82ff.

[54]Ebeling, The Problem of Historicity, 90.

unity is only absolutely necessary at the level of the local
congregation.[55] This is not to say that ecumenical dialogue
should simply cease or that alliances above the level of the
congregation do not exist. Christians can continue to seek
unity without failing to take doctrinal differences seriously. But enforced unity above the level of the congregation,
based on formal Church law, would be an inauthentic source
of unity.[56] It would endanger the free critical voice of
the Gospel and thus undermine the hermeneutical responsibility of Christianity in its continuing reappropriation of
Scripture and Church doctrine.

A summary of the main lines of Ebeling's critique of
Catholic hermeneutic may now be attempted. In Ebeling's
opinion, there is an essential incompatibility between the
Catholic understanding of tradition, on the one hand, and
critical historical awareness and hermeneutic, on the other.
The central problem is the Catholic understanding of the
actualization of revelation. Revelation is so identified by
Catholicism with the present forms of its mediation that the
historicity or "pastness" of revelation in a textual tradition is lost. The Church and its authoritative doctrinal
teaching, in particular, eliminate the need for authentic

---

[55]WF, 115-117. Reinhard Kösters maintains that the
second and third centuries were closer to being centuries of
Christian unity than Ebeling is willing to recognize.
"Dogma und Bekenntnis bei Gerhard Ebeling," Catholica 24
(1970), 51-66.

[56]WF, 182.

reappropriation and interpretation of the textual sources of faith. The "meaning" of Scripture and tradition is decided finally in Catholicism not hermeneutically but on jurisdictional grounds; continuity between faith and its origins is secured by reference to formal authority rather than by the path of interpretation itself. Theological and exegetical determinations of the meaning of texts are subservient finally to a higher authority which decides the "true" meaning in a manner oblivious to the demands of hermeneutical integrity. Moreover, an a priori impossibility of any tension between this traditional organ of interpretation and Scripture itself makes impossible any real criticism of Church teaching on the basis of Scripture or the Gospel. Rather than standing under the Word of God, the Church and its dogmas have, in effect, replaced it.

No attempt has been made at this point to provide a thorough presentation of Ebeling's hermeneutic. Some of the key distinctions which he sees between Catholic and Protestant approaches to the hermeneutical problem have, however, been presented. The Protestant principle of sola scriptura eliminates the need for an authoritative guide to interpretation, Scripture is its own guide to interpretation, possessing a "clarity" which guarantees its understandability and soteriological efficacy in any particular age and which frees it from the weight and distortion of a binding dogmatic tradition. The clarity of Scripture rests finally not in the letter, however, but in the inner subject matter or content--

the Word of God itself. The historical meaning of the text
may be unclear and even frustrate encounter with the Gospel.
Criticism of the text in light of the subject matter is thus
possible and at times even necessary. Revision and even
rejection of the letter of Scripture and tradition is a part
of responsible remembrance. Neither Scripture nor tradition
qualifies automatically as Word of God or revelation; both
bring the Christian gospel to expression only as a product
of ever-renewed interpretation. The authority of Scripture
and tradition is directly tied to their capacity to speak
savingly as Word of God in the event of proclamation. In
contrast to the Catholic focus on the "formal" authority of
Church teaching, Protestantism, if faithful to its Reformation heritage, can admit only a contentual or material
(sachlich) authority. The authority of Scripture and doctrine is a product of their ability to serve proclamation;
they "bind" the believer as Gospel rather than as Law.

Ebeling's emphasis on the individual conscience of the
interpreter reflects his conviction that material continuity
of Gospel, Scripture, and Tradition is a product of responsible interpretation. The absence of a "formal" continuity
places a heavy responsibility on interpretation itself; only
at the level of the individual may responsible interpretation take place. The individual interpreter can be asked
for his evidence; his interpretation can be checked and
examined. Interpretation is in this context "true" to the
extent that it convinces. It carries its own authority. It

must move between a faithful encounter with the historical pastness of the text and the concrete situation in which faith finds itself at any particular moment in history. When interpretation is tested for its formal or legal claim rather than for the adequacy of its bond to the texts of faith and to the situation of understanding, then hermeneutic responsibility, in any proper sense of the word, has been cast aside. The Catholic location of the final court of appeal in interpretation in the magisterium, the apparent importance of dogmatic considerations in the interpretation of Scripture, and the formal authority of dogma are all escapes from the hermeneutical problem.

III. Tradition and Hermeneutic in Catholic Thought

The focus of Ebeling's critique is the Catholic concept of tradition. Ebeling contends that revelation is actualized by Catholicism in its tradition in a way which undermines the historical bond to the textual sources of faith. This problem is most apparent for Ebeling in the case of those traditional texts which have the status of dogma. Catholic dogma by its very nature is an escape from the hermeneutical problem; its formal authority frees it both from authentic historical investigation and from critical assessment in light of Scripture. What is yet to be determined is whether Ebeling is correct in his judgment of the essential incompatibility of Catholicism with historical awareness and hermeneutic in their modern forms. Our approach to this question will be, first, to examine some of the basic forms assumed by a Catholic theology of tradition in the past. Our purpose will be to suggest that these classical approaches to the problem of tradition are open to Ebeling's critique and that contemporary Catholic theology, recognizing the historical and hermeneutical inadequacies of the classical outlook, is currently reformulating the Catholic concept of tradition. In the next chapter, Catholic approaches to the specific problem of interpreting dogmatic statements will be examined and some of the same inadequacies of the classical Catholic theology of tradition pointed out. The remaining chapters contain the major thrust of this study: the formulation of a hermeneutic of dogma which draws on the contemporary philosophical and Protestant hermeneutical discussions and which avoids the ambiguities of earlier Catholic hermeneutic.

Catholicism has never simply identified post-biblical tradition with revelation. Revelation, in the consistent teaching of the Church, received its normative expression in the apostolic period in the canon of scriptural writings.[57]

---

[57]Michael Schmaus summarizes the mainstream of Catholic teaching in this way: "Thus Scripture always remains the norm of true self-understanding for the Church. Scripture itself, however, is no longer subject to any other norm. It is, as we say, the norma normans non normata. Fundamentally this thesis means simply that Christ, present in Holy Scripture, is the norm of the Church, a norm not subject to any other norm. In this conviction, Protestant and Catholic theology agree." Dogma, vol. I (New York: Sheed and Ward, 1968), p. 205.

The problem of development of doctrine springs from this recognition of the historicity of revelation. Theories of development attempt to link dogmatic tradition to the scriptural
testimony, for the assertion that dogma expresses a truth
of "revelation" makes such a link necessary. Edward
Schillebeeckx has observed that the locus of the hermeneutical problem in Catholicism has been the question of development of doctrine. Dogma is rooted in its own historical
situation and yet somehow expresses the "same" content of
faith as Scripture itself.[58] The location of the one meaning uniting Scriptural texts and dogma constitutes the hermeneutical problem. Although the process of development of
doctrine has often been conceived in an a-historical manner,
the assertion of a once-for-all revelation and of the need to
maintain continuity with it are central elements in Catholic
faith.

A problem exists not so much in the theoretical assertion of the normativeness and historicity of revelation as
in the gap between such a theory and some of the concepts of
tradition which have emerged in the history of the Church.
At the admitted risk of oversimplification, two broad
approaches to the problem of tradition may be located in the
history of Catholic thought, both of which involve an evasion
of the hermeneutical problem. In different periods and

---

[58]Schillebeeckx, "Towards a Catholic Use of Hermeneutics," 7.

figures, a variety of one or the other of these alternatives
has provided a response to the hermeneutical problem. One
approach might be labeled the "mystical" solution and the
second the "formal-rationalist" solution. In the mystical
apprehension of tradition, the Church, Scripture, and revelation come close to being identified with one another. All
of the moments of tradition stand in a unity which breaks
down their historicity. The formal or rationalist approach
to the unity of faith appeals less to an "inner" invisible
source of continuity than to a unity of intellectual content
secured by rational or formal means. The discursive unity of
premises and conclusions, or the unity guaranteed by the formal authority of the official magisterium is appealed to.
Both the mystical and formal-rationalist variations may be
proposed simultaneously, e.g., the authority of the magisterium may rest on its special insight into a "fuller" mystical
sense of Scripture and tradition, not accessible to "secular"
reason or to the non-authoritative sources of interpretation
within the believing community. The similarity of the two
approaches to tradition is the common appeal to what Josef
Ratzinger has called a "theology of identity" (Identitätstheologie).[59] Formally, rationally, or mystically the identity of faith at all points in the history of the history of
the Church is secured. An awareness of the possibility of

_____

[59]Josef Ratzinger, Das Problem der Dogmengeschichte in
der Sicht der katholischen Theologie (Cologne: Opladen,
1966), pp. 5ff.

dialectic, discontinuity, or truly critical reappropriation
of tradition is either absent or seriously called in question.

Some concrete illustrations may make these abstract
descriptions somewhat clearer. As has been indicated,
Ebeling dates the beginning of the Catholic "escape" from
the hermeneutical problem in patristic and medieval theology.
The form this escape took was a "dehistoricization" of the
sources of faith and a growing emphasis on the presence of
revelation in the Church. A quite similar interpretation
has been provided by Yves Congar, one of the foremost historians of Catholic theology. Congar notes the same lack of
historical awareness criticized by Ebeling: an imprecision
concerning the notions of "inspiration" and "revelation"
undermined the historicity of tradition as well as a properly
historical relationship to Scripture:

> It must be recognized that the exceptionally wide
> and imprecise way in which the Middle Ages spoke
> of the "inspiration" of the Holy Spirit or of "re-
> velation" for the whole sphere of the historical
> life of the Church took insufficient account
> either of the extensive human element which helps
> to make up this sphere, or of the qualitative
> difference which must be maintained between the
> time of the prophets and apostles and that of the
> councils, Fathers, or popes.[60]

Where the modern theologian would focus on the historical
pastness and situation of a text, the Fathers and medieval
theologians sought its "typological" significance or "homo-
geneity with the heavenly reality." The inspiration marking

---

[60]_TT_, 174.

38

texts of tradition was conceived in a supratemporal context; they possessed a "suprahistoric content whose truth derived its value primarily from the fact that it was the manifesta- tion of the heavenly mystery."[61] The authority (<u>auctoritas</u>) of traditional texts was not primarily a historical cate- gory--an authority passed down from or based on continuity with an earlier period in the Church. Rather, <u>auctoritas</u> reflected the <u>function</u> or <u>status</u> of a traditional text--the place it held in the "great hierarchy of the world." Although distinguished from Scripture, the ontological sta- tus of tradition seemed at times to make it a part of <u>scriptura</u> <u>sacra</u> itself. The consequence, Congar recognizes, was a lack of historical awareness, an inadequate theory of doctrinal development, and a weakened sense of the normative importance of the apostolic witness.[62]

Despite the problematic understanding of history in patristic and early medieval theology, an emphasis on ration- al and juridical categories had not as yet entered the pic- ture. The great theologians of the medieval period distin- guished the one "authority"--the living power of the Gospel --from the numerous "authorities" in which it was contained. This inner soteriological content of tradition, and not for- mal authority, was the focus throughout the early medieval

---

[61]<u>TT</u>, 82.
[62]<u>TT</u>, 93-94.

and patristic periods.[63] The later division of Scripture and tradition into two separate "sources" of revelation was not yet a part of the Catholic outlook. Both Scripture and tradition brought to expression the one saving mystery of Christ, wholly contained in the scriptural witness and handed on in the later tradition of the Church.[64] In the twelfth century, however, the Gregorian Reform brought a decisive shift in perspective:

> The Gregorian Reform and its influence, decisive for an epoque as full of life as the twelfth century in the West, marked a definite turning point: the transition from an appreciation of the ever active presence of God to that of juridicial powers put at the free disposal of, and perhaps even handed over as property to "the Church," i.e. the hierarchy.[65]

With this process, even the latent capability of distinguishing the Gospel from the Church, and retaining it as a critical norm was called in question. Gospel and the concept of Church tended to merge together in the form of the official magisterium. Not surprisingly, subsequent reform movements appealed to the Gospel over the Church.

The contemporary split between Catholic theology and

---

[63] Walter Kasper, Die Methoden der Dogmatik (Munich: Kösel, 1966), pp. 47ff. (Eng. tr. The Methods of Dogmatic Theology (Glen Rock, N. J.: Paulist Press, 1969). Citations will be from the German edition.

[64] Richard Boeckler, Der moderne römisch-katholische Traditionsbegriff (Göttingen: Vandenhoeck and Ruprecht, 1967), p. 201.

[65] TT, 135-136.

historical consciousness is at its roots a product of the
encounter between the emerging juridicism in the Catholic
Church and the challenges of Nominalism, Humanism, and Reformation.[66] The assumed authority of tradition and unity
of faith and reason characteristic of medieval theology at
its high point disintegrated under the criticism of all three
of these movements. Nominalism reduced the tradition to
nomina, possessing no direct authority and introduced a
rational, critical outlook which sundered authority and reason. The consequent division of methods, as Walter Kasper
has pointed out, produced "a rational mathematico-scientific
method on the one hand," and "fideism, biblicism, and intuitive mysticism on the other." Reason and faith were
increasingly dissociated from one another.[67] As the tradition lost its automatic authoritative status, theology tended
to move farther and farther away from its biblical and historical origins.[68] Humanism and Reformation drove new wedges
between faith and reason in Catholic theology--humanism by
the appeal to the historical fontes behind the tradition, the
Reformers by an appeal to sola scriptura.[69] The remaining
source of unity seemed increasingly to be the claim of the

---

[66]Kasper, Die Methoden der Dogmatik, 23ff.

[67]Ibid.; cf. J. Beumer, Theologie als Glaubensverständnis (Würzburg: Echter, 1953), pp. 80-93.

[68]Kasper, Die Methoden der Dogmatik, 47-48.

[69]Ibid., 24-25.

formal authority of the tradition. Counter-Reformation
theology

> is characterized by the affirmation of the princi-
> ple of authority, that is to say the formal prin-
> ciple or quo, in a way which hardly allows for its
> conditioning by the content, the objective datum
> or quod...the force of the decisions taken by
> authority appears as unconditioned and truly divine.
> Instead of seeing tradition as having its reference
> to the past, there is a tendency to see it in
> reference to the current magisterium of the Church
> expressing itself in the passing of time.[70]

Ecclesiastical positivism and an inability to come to terms
with emerging historical awareness have marked the course of
Catholic theology since the Reformation.

The development of dogmatic theology in the seventeenth
and eighteenth centuries is particularly indicative of the
growing separation of Catholic theology and historical consciousness. In the face of Protestant and historical criticism, dogmatic theologians sought the timeless and unchanging
content of the faith. One doctrine of faith was spelled out
--a subject matter free from the relativities of history and
thus not subject to dispute.[71] The "histories" of dogma
that emerged in this period, e.g. the Annals of Baronius,
simply could not grasp the relativity and historicality of
doctrine. Instead, the identity and unhistoricality of the
content of faith was affirmed.[72] The attitude expressed by

---

[70]TT, 176.

[71]Yves Congar, The History of Theology (Garden City:
Doubleday, 1968), pp. 178-179. cf. Kasper, Die Methoden der
Dogmatik, 28-29.

[72]This emphasis on identity is noted by J. Ratzinger in
Das Problem der Dogmengeschichte, pp. 11-14.

42

Bossuet is not a-typical:

> The Church's doctrine is always the same. The
> Gospel is never different from what it was before.
> Hence, if at any time someone says that the faith
> includes something which yesterday was not said to
> be of the faith, it is always heterodoxy, which is
> any doctrine different from orthodoxy. There is no
> difficulty about recognizing false doctrine: there
> is no argument about it: it is recognized at once,
> whenever it appears, merely because it is new..."[73]

Even such an unchanging deposit of faith needs to be identified, however, and is thus in principle subject to historical criticism. The solution to this problem proposed by
Isaac Berruyer and other theologians fearful of the ambiguities and tensions of history, was to remove the need for
historical demonstration of the continuity of the faith. The
only absolute source of certainty for Berruyer was the infallible teaching authority of the Church. Once defined by
the magisterium, Church teaching enjoyed an a priori value
for faith and unity with Scripture which eliminated completely the need for historical investigation.[74]

Those post-Tridentine theologians who were unwilling to
ground the development of doctrine in such an arbitrary
appeal to formal authority did not, however, approach the
problem from an authentically historical perspective. From
the fourteenth century on, the emphasis of Catholic theology
turned to logical schemes of doctrinal development. The
movement of faith was conceived as the movement of discursive

___

[73]Bossuet, quoted in Owen Chadwick, From Bossuet to
Newman. The Idea of Doctrinal Development (Cambridge:
Cambridge University Press, 1957), pp. 23ff.

[74]Ibid., 72-73.

thought, connecting revealed truths with conclusions of later
theology. The major points of contention dividing theologians and schools remained within the logical arena; they
expounded different views of the premises required to arrive
at a revealed conclusion.[75] Vasquez and Molina, for example,
were at odds over the binding character of a conclusion
derived from a combination of "revealed" and "morally certain" premises. For Vasquez, such a conclusion was revealed;
for Molina, it was not.[76] This rationalist approach to
development influenced a major segment of nineteenth century
thought as well as the thinking of many Catholic theologians
in this century. It is only in the last few decades that it
has suffered a near total eclipse. The complete scope of
the recent critical reaction to logical schemes of development
cannot be presented in detail here.[77] Common to such criticism, however, is the recognition of the lack of historical
awareness. Revelation is conceived in logical theories as a

---

[75] For extended discussions of the theories of development
propounded in this period, see Chadwick, From Bossuet to
Newman, 23ff. and H. Hammans, Die neueren katholischen
Erklärungen der Dogmenentwicklung (Essen: Ludgerus, 1965),
pp. 13-21.

[76] Chadwick, From Bossuet to Newman, 32-33.

[77] For examples of such criticism see Karl Rahner, "The
Development of Dogma," Theological Investigations, vol. I
(Baltimore: Helicon, 1961; Rahner, "Dogmenentwicklung," in
Mysterium Salutis, I, ed. by Johannes Feiner and Magnus Lohrer
(Einsiedeln: Benziger, 1965), pp. 756-765; F. Lakner, "Zur
Frage der Definibilität einer geoffenbarten Wahrheit," ZKT 85
(1963), 322-338; E. Schillebeeckx, Revelation and Theology,
vol. I (New York: Sheed and Ward, 1967), pp. 66-67; and
Hammans, Dogmenentwicklung 164-173.

summary of timeless principles or as a dead deposit of truths in the distant past which the Church speculatively reappropriates from a great historical distance. A more positive estimate of the mediating function of history in the development of dogma is lacking.

The nineteenth century marks a rebirth of the mystical approach to tradition and a significant departure from the rationalism of post-Tridentine Catholic theology. A new understanding of doctrinal development and of tradition emerged most noticeably in the Tübingen school of Johann Adam Möhler, Johann von Drey, and Johann Kuhn.[78] An openness to the intellectual currents of the early nineteenth century and a willingness to rethink Catholic tradition in light of the new cultural milieu gave the Tübingen theologians the impetus for renewal. Romanticism, in particular, contributed an understanding of tradition as Erlebnis, the organic unity of lived Christian experience.[79] For the Tübingen theolo-

---

[78]One of the best short surveys of the movement of nineteenth century theology is that of Bernhard Welte, "Zum Struktur wandel der katholischen Theologie im 19. Jahrhundert," in Auf der Spur des Ewigen (Freiburg: Herder, 1965), pp. 380-409. To the names of Möhler, Drey and Kuhn, Welte adds Franz Anton Staudenmeier, Johann Baptist Hirsher, Johann Michael Sailer, Franz von Baader, Martin Deutinger, Georg Hermes and Anton Günther as being figures of importance in the theological renewal. The best full length treatments of the Tübingen school may be found in the works of Josef Rupert Geiselmann. See, in particular, his Die katholische Tübinger Schule (Freiburg: Herder, 1964).

[79]For discussions of the Tübingen understanding of tradition see Hamanns, Dogmenentwicklung, 25ff.; and Geiselmann, Die Tübinger Schule, 77-88.

gians, the continuity of faith was grounded in the historical
life-process of the Church, and not in a static system of
propositional truths. The simple pre-reflective grasp of God
in Christian faith was identified by Möhler and his successors
as the foundation of Christian history. Although rational
elucidations of faith were accepted as a necessary part of
faith, such attempts at expression never fully encapsulated
the lived experience of the Christian mystery. A conception
of development in terms of lived Christian experience per-
mitted the Tübingen theologians to draw connections between
the movement of faith and the movement of history. Growth
and even dialectic were not rejected automatically as distortions of faith, but were seen as the necessary consequence of
its historicality. The unity of faith rested in the psychological unity of the Church in all ages produced by the saving
event of Christ, and not in a rationally demonstrable unchanging deposit of propositional terms.[80]

   Just as in patristic and medieval theology, the focus on

---

[80]Geiselmann, Die Tübinger Schule, 77-78. Welte describes
the changed understanding of tradition in this way: "...in
allen diesen Untersuchungen (scil. the renewed theology of the
early nineteenth century) finden wir die Bemühung, den Begriff
der Überlieferung totaler und zentraler zu fassen als nur in
der Weise, darin eine abstrakte Wiedergabe oder Bewegung
abstrakter Gedenken zu sehen. Immer wieder wird Tradition zum
Begriff der lebendigen Totalität des christlichen Daseins aus
dem Geiste des Herrn, welches Dasein als solches Leben und also
schen im Stande der Unmittelbarkeit und nicht erst in dem der
Reflexion immer wieder Leben weckt und darin die Einheit des
Geistes in der lebendigen Mannigfaltigkeit der immer weiter
fortschreitenden Geschichte gewährleistet." "Zum Strukturwandel der katholischen Theologie im 19. Jahrhundert," in Auf der
Spur des Ewigen, p. 392.

the living, present mystery of Christ in the Church carried

the possibility of a deemphasis of the normative historical-

ity and pastness of Scripture. At times Möhler seemed to

identify Church and Scripture.[81] Kuhn carefully separated

"scientific" interpretation of Scripture from "dogmatic"

interpretation. Only the latter, through the magisterium or

subjective faith interpretation of the believer, could ground

development of doctrine. The "presuppositionless" approach

of critical historical exegesis exempted it from the beginning

from a real encounter with the mystery of faith. Just as in

the rationalist forms of Catholic theology, Tübingen theology

found it difficult to unite dogmatic and historical method-

ology. The continuing psychological unity of Christianity,

interpreted in the context of a Romantic "Geist" metaphysic

provided an inadequate foundation for a hermeneutic con-

ceived in properly historical terms.[82] An indication of this

intrinsic inadequacy may be pointed out in the development

of Möhler's thought. In his early writings, the Romantic

notion of the inner Geist of Christianity provided Möhler

---

[81]Both Boeckler, Der moderne römisch-katholische Traditionsbegriff, 171-172 and Peter Lengsfeld, Überlieferung und
Schrift in der evangelischen und katholischen Theologie der
Gegenwart (Paderborn: Bonifacius, 1960), pp. 108ff. have
expressed this criticism.

[82]At a later point in this study, it will be suggested
that the same difficulty afflicts the Romantic hermeneutic of
the Geisteswissenschaften in the neneteenth century. The
modern hermeneutical discussion in philosophy and theology has
emerged from the critique of Romantic hermeneutic in light of
the historicality of human existence.

with his principle for unifying the historical continuum of
Christian faith. The Symbolik and other later writings,
however, contain a new stress on the historical multiplicity
and even contradiction of the forms of the "inner" life of
Christianity. When tradition is historically perceived, a
naive assumption of unity is called in question. Möhler's
way out of this dilemma followed a path quite similar to the
scholasticism of his century; he emphasized the formal authority of the magisterium as an arbiter of conflicts of interpretation. In the interpretation of the teaching authority of the Church, the certain and "true" meaning of the
faith may be located.[83] The sudden threat of historicism,
raised by the new openness of Tübingen theology to history
and the hermeneutic problem, carried with it obvious dangers
which were answered by an appeal to authority.

In the last half of the nineteenth century, Catholic
theology turned away from the insights of the Tübingen theologians and back to the rationalism of an earlier time.
Johann Baptist Hirsher, Franz Anton Staudenmeier and other remaining representatives of the theological renewal of the
early part of the century were pushed to the fringes of theological thought.[84] A central part of the change of theological climate was the triumph of Neoscholasticism. Particularly after the canonization of Thomas' theology by Leo XIII,

---

[83]Geiselmann, Die Tübinger Schule, 81-86.

[84]Welte, "Zum Strukturwandel der katholischen Theologie,"
318.

48

Scholastic method dominated the theological scene.[85] Tübingen theology had sought a new encounter between Catholic
theology and historical awareness; Neoscholasticism returned,
instead, to the defensive and polemical outlook of the
seventeenth and eighteenth centuries. In the face of critical historical work on the Bible and Church history, theologians reaffirmed the necessity for a stable content of faith
elevated above the flux and movement of history.[86]

The disputes between the German and Roman schools of
Catholic theology in the nineteenth century revolved around
the problem of reconciling orthodox scholastic theology and
historical thought. While it would be a mistake simply to
label the Roman school as "antihistorical," the question
that divided the Roman and German schools, and one that has

---

[85]Walter Kasper, Die Methoden der Dogmatik, 26-27 describes the change in this way: "Katholische Rechtgläubigkeit
und scholastische Methode schienen identisch zu sein; und
damit schienen sich das modernegeschichtliche Denken und der
katholische Glaube von vornherein zu widersprechen. Das Problem der Geschichtlichkeit der Wahrheit, wie es die Humanisten
stellten, und das Problem der Kirchlichkeit der Theologie, wie
es durch die Reformatoren gestellt war, waren damit in unseli-
ger Weise miteinander verknüpft."

[86]Welte, "Zum Strukturwandel der katholischen Theologie,"
402. "Die Theologie fand Anlass, den Glauben tunlichst dis-
sozierend von diesem infragestellenden und unruhigen Element
abzutrennen und nun ihrerseits mehr und mehr von der Seite
darzustellen, von der es sich als ein zeitlos System darbietat,
Die Theologie versuchte das immer Gleiche und Unveränlichte zu
erheben und damit die metaphysche Konzeption des Christentums
vor seinem geschichtlichen Charakter in den Vordergrund zu
rücken."

persisted into the twentieth century, was how to reconcile universally valid truth with historical awareness.[87] The desire to defend the absolute truth of Christian faith pushed Roman theology into an overemphasis of the official magisterium of the Church. Perrone, the first major representative of the Roman school, could locate the certainty of faith only in the infallibly guaranteed teaching of the magisterium.[88] The historical distance of Scripture, the "remote" rule of faith, necessitated an infallible "proximate" rule of interpretation in order to secure the certainty of faith. In Perrone, and in the later theology of Passaglia and Schrader, the role of the laity was deemphasized. The community "sense of faith" was primarily an echo of the real organ of tradition, the hierarchical magisterium. Revelation is the body of propositional truths handed over to the teaching office of the Church and from it, especially from the Pope, to the Church as a whole.[89] In the authority conscious decades at the end of the nineteenth century, the defense of papal authority became a primary theological concern. The tradition expressed by Rome and the hierarchical magisterium as a whole stood for Roman theology in unquestioned unity with the

[87]Kasper, Die Methoden der Dogmatik, 27-28. cf. Kasper, Die Lehre von der Tradition in der Römischen Schule (Freiburg: Herder, 1962).

[88]Kasper, Die Lehre von der Tradition, 51ff.; 66-67.

[89]Kasper, Die Lehre von der Tradition, 132-133. The charism of infallibility also rests initially with the Pope and then passes from him to the Church as a whole. (133-134).

apostolic witness. This apologetic need to guarantee the one unchanging tradition throughout the history of the Church endangered the use of critical historical method. As in earlier periods, dogmatic and historical method moved away from one another.[90] Moreover, it is difficult in Roman theology to distinguish Scripture, tradition, and Gospel. Perrone's concept of tradition, for example, as Walter Kasper points out, "allows a theoretical but no longer a practical and concrete distinction in the life of the Church between traditio divina and traditio humana.[91] Passaglia and Schrader, according to Kasper, never simply identified tradition with the teaching office of the Church. The function of the magisterium is for both one of interpretation. No new revelation may be found in the teaching of the Church, only authoritative witness to the revelation contained in Scripture. Word of God was properly for Passaglia and Schrader the Christ-event itself, normatively witnessed to in Scripture and "remembered" by the Church.[92] As in the case of Perrone, however, it is difficult to combine the Roman school's overriding sense of magisterial authority with the concrete possibility of in-

---

[90] This separation of theological methods is a reoccurring theme in Kasper's study of the main figures in the Roman school. See, e.g., Die Lehre von der Tradition, 336-337.

[91] Kasper, Die Lehre von der Tradition, 172, 178-181. "Die entscheidende Schwierigkeit dieses Überlieferungsbegriffes besteht darin, dass es sich bei ihm zwar noch theoretisch, aber nicht mehr praktisch und konkret im Leben der Kirche unterscheiden lässt zwischen traditio divina und tradition humana."

[92] Ibid., 351-352; 394-395.

terpretations that may expand and possibly even correct
magisterial teaching. The freedom of interpretation as a
whole, the critical power of the Gospel, and the free conscience of the individual interpreter are closely allied.
Only in this context, is responsible hermeneutic possible.
Without such guarantees of the freedom of theology, an appeal
to the purely "interpretative" function of the magisterium
has little real content. The task suggested at the beginning
of this survey, the development of a Catholic hermeneutic
which combines authority and historical method, remained in
the Roman school an uncompleted task.

Many of the concerns of the Tübingen theologians were
resurrected in the Modernist controversy at the turn of the
century. For the first time, the hermeneutical problem was
brought clearly into focus in Catholic theology. By the end
of the nineteenth century it had become apparent that critical historical methodology was a permanent feature of the
modern mind. Alfred Loisy and the other modernists took as
a key task the integration of this historical awareness with
Catholic faith. Loisy, for example, proposed a complete revision of Catholic theology in the light of historical re-
search. He recognized that faith and Christian truth extended
beyond the data that historical method could provide. But if
the historical life of Christ or other events in Scripture
were the object of investigation, then Loisy believed that
critical history was the only avenue to knowledge. As testi-
monies to the course of history, the Gospels could only be

treated like any other historical source.[93]

The reaction of Maurice Blondel to Loisy's program provided the clearest statement of the problem of history and
faith in the modern period. His reflections on the hermeneutical function of tradition were developed from a thoroughly
worked out philosophical foundation and possess a comprehen-
siveness and depth previously unrealized in Catholic
thought.[94] Blondel was particularly troubled by the relationship of "Christian facts" (history) and "Christian beliefs" (dogma). In the Catholic discussion of his period,
Blondel located two extreme approaches to the relationship,
neither of which was acceptable. "Extrinsicism," characteristic of scholastic method, simply proceeded oblivious to
historical reality, operating freely with principles and conclusions which were only remotely related to history itself.[95]
Such an approach was only possible, Blondel believed, in a
period when historical knowledge was lacking, and dogmatics
could stand on its own artificially created historical foundation. The advance of historical investigation in the nineteenth century had removed such a possibility. The second
approach to history, which was as threatening to authentic

---

[93] Alfred Loisy, quoted in René Marlé, *Au coeur de la
crise moderniste. Le dossier inédit d'une controverse.*
(Paris: Montaigne, 1960), p. 100.

[94] *Ibid.*, 98.

[95] Maurice Blondel, *History and Dogma* (New York: Holt,
Rinehart and Winston, 1964), pp. 107, 226ff.

faith as extrinsicism, was the "historicism" characteristic of Loisy. Historicism sought to ground faith and dogma on what the "objective" historian could perceive as the real course of historical events; e.g., on what could be learned about the "real" pattern of Christ's life. The historicist outlook suffered, Blondel believed, from a number of inadequacies. In the first place, it was philosophically naive. The "objective" historian proceeded unaware of the raft of prejudices and presuppositions which molded his interpretation.[96] History is always a "construction" or "imaginative picture" and cannot be simply identified with the reality of past historical phenomena.[97] More importantly, however, historicists overlooked the living reality of Christian tradition in favor of abstract and lifeless facts of history. The lived reality and fullness of Christian faith always transcends what the historian can perceive of the events of the past; critical history is simply inadequate to bear the full weight of Christian tradition.[98] Both extrinsicism and historicism arrive at conclusions which are exterior to the real history of faith.

Blondel's analysis of the inadequacies of extrinsicism and historicism clearly revealed, as he saw it, the need for

---

[96] Blondel, History and Dogma, 109, 236-237.

[97] Ibid., 109, 298ff.

[98] Ibid., 110, 240-241.

an "intermediary" between history and dogma. He found such
an intermediary in the living tradition of faith. The "real"
Christ is more for Blondel than a theological abstraction or
an objectively perceived figure of the past. He is the continuing active source of life in the Church. It is only from
within the circle of faith, from the actual faith experience
of the Church, that proper apprehension of history can take
place. Even the text of Scripture as a literary presentation
of the historical events in the early Church cannot be simply
identified with this living tradition. The historical influence of Christ "inaugurated a tradition of devotion and adora-
tion which Christian literature neither exhausts nor fully
represents, even when closest to its source."[99] The full
reality of tradition is more than a deposit of truths stated
once for all in the apostolic period; through the continuing
encounter with Christ truths are formulated which reexpress
the living reality of apostolic faith without being explicitly
linked to the scriptural testimony. In his own "philosophy
of action" Blondel found a way of clarifying the movement from
the prereflective lived experience of faith to clearly formulated knowledge.[100] Rationalist approaches to doctrinal
development overlooked the priority of prereflective lived
experience by seeking a pattern of history in harmony with
discursive thought. The real historical path of faith is from

---

[99] Blondel, History and Dogma, 111, 247, 268.

[100] Ibid., 272.

faith to dogma rather than from dogma to faith.[101] An "intermediary" between history and dogma, different from rationalist syllogism and the objective facts of critical history
had been found: "The synthesis [of history and dogma] lies
neither in the facts, nor in the ideas alone, but in the Tradition which embraces within it the facts of history, the
effort of reason, and the accumulated experiences of the faithful."[102]

Blondel's History and Dogma anticipates some of the themes
of the contemporary hermeneutical discussion. The distinction
drawn between Christian tradition perceived from the standpoint of critical historical method and tradition embodied in
the living experience of faith has reappeared in a variety of
forms. There is a difference between the events of the
Christian past perceived purely in their own historical situations and the handing on of these events as concerns of faith
today. Both Protestantism and Catholicism have felt the need
to move beyond the "letter" of Christian texts. The "facts"
of Christian history are remembered and appropriated in the
context of their significance for faith in the present in a
way which takes them beyond the sphere of interest of critical historical method.

Contemporary hermeneutic, however, is marked by a concern to ground the "subjective" apprehension of history in
a method and thus not leave it to intuition or mystical ex-

---

[101]Blondel, History and Dogma, 279, 274ff.

[102]Ibid., 269.

perience. This concern points to a dimension of the hermeneutic problem which is inadequately treated by Blondel. It
is not clear in Blondel's writings whether "tradition" is
any longer legitimately an object of historical investigation
in any proper sense of the word. Like Tübingen theology before him, Blondel finds it difficult to combine a recognition of the living presence of tradition with a recognition
of its historicality. What precisely is the importance of
the historical meaning of traditional and scriptural texts
to faith? How do historical knowledge and method function
in Christian dogmatics? These questions are not satisfac-
torily answered in History and Dogma, and the reason is not
hard to find. Blondel separates historical knowing and the
concerns of faith because he begins with an inadequate understanding of history. The notion of history attacked by
Blondel, and that which seems to define history and historical knowledge as he understood them, is clearly in the positivistic vein of eighteenth and early nineteenth century
thought. History "as it really was," perceived presupposition-
lessly, without any dogmatic interest, is the model called in
question by Blondel. But is this description of historical
understanding either accurate or complete? A central theme
of contemporary hermeneutic has been a critique of historical
positivism and an effort to define a broader concept of
history which unites the past perceived from the standpoint of
critical-historical method and the past perceived in terms of
its existential significance. What form this redefinition has
taken and its implications for Catholic theology and hermeneu-

tic remain to be clarified.

Some of the ambiguities in Blondel's thought might have been eliminated and a more fruitful encounter of Catholic thought and historical awareness made possible if the debates initiated in the Modernist period had been carried on. But discussion was brought to an abrupt halt by the papal condemnations of 1907.[103] Subsequent restrictions imposed by the magisterium prevented any real reemergence of the problem of history and faith until the nineteen forties and fifties. In the last three decades, Catholic theology has demonstrated a renewed interest in historical awareness and its implications for faith and theology. Past magisterial opposition to critical historical method, particularly in the field of biblical interpretation, has been left behind as a relic of another age. With the movement toward a commonly accepted historical approach to Scripture, inter-confessional cooperation in biblical exegesis has become commonplace. Unfortunately, the rapprochement of Catholic systematic and dogmatic theology with historical awareness is in a much earlier stage of development. It is now clear that the older forms of an unbroken, non-historical relationship to tradition are no longer acceptable.[104] A clear feature of post-Vatican II theology is a concern to unite the splintered methods of historical and dogmatic theology.[105] As Eberhard Simons has observed, however, this inte-

---

[103]DS., 3401-3466, 3825f.

[104]Josef Duss-von Werdt, Theologie aus Glaubenserfahrung (Zurich: Benziger, 1969), p. 9.

[105]Kasper, Die Methoden der Dogmatik, 10.

58

gration of methods, as well as the related dialogue of exegesis and dogmatics, is a task of the future.[106] No commonly accepted solution to the fundamental hermeneutical problem of Catholic systematic theology has been reached. This is nowhere more apparent, as the next chapter will indicate, than in the interpretation of dogma.

What is at stake in the current shift of Catholic theological method, as Bernard Lonergan has forcefully emphasized, is a change in scientific ideals. The importance assigned by scholastic theology to metaphysical necessity and certainty has been replaced by a new openness to historicality, empirical method, and the probability of all theological results.[107] The certain principles drawn from the authorities or sources of systematic theology have been recast in a historical light where the question of their "meaning" properly emerges. Logical manipulation of propositions, so evident in classical approaches to the development of doctrine is now more clearly recognized to be inappropriate to a discipline which, like the other human sciences, takes human experience and history as its field of investigation.

One important consequence of the new openness of Catholic theology to historical awareness has been a reformulation of the concept of tradition. The full scope of this reformula-

---

[106]Eberhard Simons, "Die Bedeutung der Hermeneutik,"184-185.

[107]Bernard Lonergan, Doctrinal Pluralism (Milwaukee: Marquette University Press, 1971), pp. 4ff. cf. Lonergan, "Theology in its New Context," in Theology of Renewal, vol.I, ed. by L. K. Shook (New York: Herder, 1968), pp. 34-46.

tion cannot be presented in this study, although those aspects which touch on the problem of interpreting dogma will be more carefully examined in subsequent chapters. Above all, historical awareness has brought a clearer apprehension of the historicality of traditional texts. All of the authoritative texts of faith, those of Scripture and of post-biblical tradition, emerge, are handed on, and are reappropriated in changing historical situations. The historical particularity of all of these levels of tradition must be recognized and incorporated in an adequate hermeneutical theory. A further consequence of the new Catholic appreciation of historicality is a distinction of the multiple "traditions" of faith from the one tradition or Gospel of Christianity. A new awareness of the legitimate features of the Protestant principle of sola scriptura as well as a renewed investigation of the relationship of dogma and gospel spring from this recognition. What has become most apparent is that the acceptance of historicality calls in question the "theology of identity" of earlier periods. As the brief historical survey of Catholic concepts of tradition has indicated, both the "mystical" and "formal-rationalist" approaches to tradition produced an inability to come to terms with historical thought. Both involved a dehistoricization of tradition. They have been treated in some detail because they have exerted influence on the interpretation of those elements of the tradition which are the dogmas of the Church. In the next chapter, an examination of some of the classical approaches to the hermeneutic of dogma will indicate a number of ways in which the historicality of dogma also has been devalued. The ambiguities of earlier attitudes toward tradition reappear on occasion even in recent studies of the problem of dogma. This suggests the necessity for a reassessment of the hermeneutic of dogma--one which takes account of the problem of historicality and of the Protestant and philosophical hermeneutical discussions of the modern period.

CHAPTER II

DOGMA AND THE HERMENEUTIC PROBLEM

I. Dogma and Historical Awareness

The history of the Catholic Church in the post-Tridentine period is marked by a continuing conflict with historical awareness and method. The movement from a static-
essentialist view of reality to an appreciation of process,
change, and relativity has appeared as a threat to the truth
and identity of Catholic faith. A main line of response to
this challenge of history has been the formulation of notions
of Catholic tradition which have sought to guarantee the
continuity and truth of faith by raising it, in a variety of
ways, above the movement of history. A "theology of identity," conceived in mystical or formal-rational terms, has
delayed a full reconciliation of Catholic theology with historical method and contemporary hermeneutic. Understandably,
those elements of tradition embodying the strongest and
clearest claim to absolute, unchanging truth--the dogmas of
the Church--have been a main focus of this clash of Catholic
faith and historical awareness. When the certitude of dogma
has seemed to be threatened by historical criticism, the reaction of the Church, as the Modernist crisis illustrates,
has been quick and harsh. Ebeling is correct in his assertion that dogma, by its very nature, has often been portrayed

61

as a "solution" to the hermeneutical problem. The forms
such a solution have taken will be examined in this chapter
following a consideration of the Catholic concept of dogma
in its present form and in its historical background.

The first Vatican Council provided the currently
accepted definition of dogma: "Further all those things
are to be believed with divine and Catholic faith which are
contained in the word of God, written or handed down, and
which the Church, either by a solemn judgment, or by her
ordinary and universal magisterium, proposes for belief as
having been divinely revealed."[1] Two elements are contained in the conciliar definition: Dogma is a statement
of revealed truth, formally defined as such by the Church.
It expresses the conviction that the Church does not live
purely by reflection upon her inner experience, but in remembrance of and continuity with a historical revelation.
It further expresses the conviction that such remembrance is

---

[1]Neuner-Roos 90, DS 3011. "Porro fide divina et catholica ea omnia credenda sunt, quae in verbo Dei scripto vel
tradito continentur et ab Ecclesia sive solemni iudicio sive
ordinario et universali magisterio tanquam divinitus revelata
credenda propununter." cf. CIC 1322-1323. For a more recent
theological definition of dogma in the pattern of the Vatican
statement see Karl Rahner and Karl Lehmann, Kerygma and Dogma
(New York: Herder, 1969), p. 38. "Thus the two essential
elements in the idea of dogma...are first, the express and
definitive declaration by the Church that a certain statement
is a revealed truth and second, the inter-relatedness of this
expressed truth to the divine, official and public Christian
revelation...and thus the fact that it is contained in the
Word of God as it comes to us in Scripture and/or Tradition."
cf. the definition by Walter Kasper, Dogma unter dem Wort
Gottes (Mainz: Grünewald, 1966), pp. 25ff.

properly social and not solely individual in character.
Dogmas must be identified clearly and specifically by the
magisterium acting for the Church as a whole. Two processes
of recognition are possible: 1) teachings have dogmatic
status which represent the consensus fidei in the everyday
preaching and teaching of the Church and which are taught as
truths revealed by God; 2) "extraordinary" definitions of
dogma are also possible in general councils and in papal
decisions ex cathedra in which the pope speaks as a representative of the whole Church.[2] The definition of infallibility
at Vatican I focused on these latter solemn papal decisions:
"the Roman pontiff...is possessed of that infallibility with
which the Divine Redeemer willed that his Church should be
endowed for defining doctrine regarding faith and morals...
therefore such definitions of the Roman pontiff are irreformable of themselves, and not from the consent of the Church."[3]
The precise content of this infallibility was not clarified
by Vatican I and is the subject of a debate in contemporary

---

[2]B. Gasser, Mansi 52, 123c; cf. Kasper, Dogma unter dem
Wort Gottes, 26; and Rahner-Lehmann, Kerygma and Dogma, 37-38.

[3]Neuner-Roos 388, DS 3074. "Romanum Pontificem, cum ex
cathedra loquitur, id est, cum omnium Christianorum pastoris
et doctoris munere fungens pro suprema sua Apostolica auctor-
itate doctrinam de fide vel moribus ab universa Ecclesia te-
nendam definit, per assistentiam divinam ipsi in beato Petro
promissam, ea infallibilitate pollere, qua divinus Redemptor
Ecclesiam suam in definienda doctrina de fide vel moribus in-
structam esse voluit; ideoque eiusmodi Romani Pontificis de-
finitiones ex sese, non autem ex consensu Ecclesiae, irre-
formabiles esse."

Catholic theology which will be discussed in the last chapter of this study. It should be noted now, however, that papal infallibility is linked to the infallibility of the Church as a whole, and that dogmatic definitions are interpretations of a historical revelation.

These last qualifications, as we have seen, are not enough for Gerhard Ebeling. The "irreformable" quality of definitions, their binding authority, the role of teaching authority in identifying dogma, and other aspects of Catholic dogma constitute, in Ebeling's opinion, a flight from the hermeneutical problem. Formal authority, a court of law, rather than a critical and honest process of interpretation, identifies the meaning and truth of dogmatic texts. The expression of the Christian revelation in dogma is not the product of a constantly renewed act of interpretation, but rather a static possession or law--the product of a judicial decision. Dogma, in the Catholic understanding, requires a "special" hermeneutic--one which evades the tensions of history and one which is incompatible with authentic historical and hermeneutical awareness. With this criticism in mind, our task now will be to examine the Catholic concept of dogma and some of the classical approaches to its interpretation. Our thesis will be that, as in the case of Catholic concepts of tradition, ways of interpreting dogma have emerged in Catholic theology which, do, in fact, contradict historical awareness and hermeneutical integrity. Just as contemporary Catholic theology has been marked by a concern to reformulate

the concept of tradition in light of the hermeneutical problem, a similar reformulation is appropriate in the case of
dogma. A first step to such a reformulation is to look more
closely at the concept of dogma expressed at Vatican I as it
came to define the character of post-Vatican theology. Our
focus will be first on the historical background of the
definition, and then on the main terms of the definition itself.

II. Changes in the Concept of Dogma

The history of the notion of dogma reveals a number of
meanings of the term not emphasized in the definition at
Vatican I or in subsequent theology. Our purpose is not a
comprehensive analysis of the history of the notion of dogma,
but an indication of some transformations in its meaning
which are particularly important in a reinterpretation of
the problem of dogma in light of hermeneutic. A major impetus toward a renewed understanding of dogma and of the process of its interpretation has been the recovery of some of
these forgotten elements of tradition.[4] Although the word

---

[4]For a penetrating analysis of the history of the
changes in the concept of dogma and an attempt to reappropriate the insights of earlier tradition, see Walter Kasper,
Dogma unter dem Wort Gottes. Other important historical works
on the concept of dogma are A. Deneffe, "Dogma. Wort und
Begriff," Scholastik 6 (1931), 381-400; RAC, III, 1257-1260
(Ranft, I semasiologisch); RGG, II, 221-222 (Gloege); HthG, I,
225-230 (Geiselmann); E. Schlink, "Die Struktur der dogmatischen Aussage als Oekumenisches Problem," Kerygma und Dogma 3
(1957), 251-306; Johannes Beumer, "'Res fidei et morum':
Die Entwicklung eines theologischen Begriffs in den Dekreten
der drei letzten Ökumenischen Konzilien," Annuarium
Historiae Conciliorum 2 (1970), 112-134; Maurice Bévenot,

dogma occurs in the New Testament, it is not employed in the sense defined by Vatican I. In its appearances in Scripture, "dogma" has the meaning of an imperial or royal edict (Lk. 21:1; Acts 17:7; Hebrews 11:23); a norm set by the Apostolic Council (Acts 15:22; 15:28; 16:4); or a law of the Old Testament (Eph. 2:15; Col. 2:14.[5] Walter Kasper has noted that the decision concerning the Gentile mission and the relationship of law and gospel (Acts 15) bears an "indirect" relationship to modern dogma. A decision was taken which proved to be constitutive for the Church as a whole. A choice was made which signified a freedom in the Church, and a willingness to make new decisions in the Holy Spirit. Kasper recognizes, however, that the decision produced neither a "binding" confession nor a teaching in the modern sense.[6] Those parts of Scripture which come closest to the modern definition of dogma are not the "dogmas" of the New Testament, but rather the creedal formulations

---

"'Faith and Morals' in the Councils of Trent and Vatican One." Heythrop Journal 3 (1962), 15-30; J. David, "Glaube und Sitten: eine missverständliche Formel," Orientisrung 35 (1971), 32-34; Piet Fransen, "Réflexions sur l'anathème au concile de Trente," ETL 29 (1953), 657-672; Albert Lang, "Der Bedeutungswandel der Begriffe 'fides' und 'haeresis' und die dogmatische Wertung der Konzilentscheidungen von Vienne und Trient," MthZ 4 (1953), 133-146; A. Lang, Die theologische Prinzipienlehr der mittelalterlichen Scholastik (Freiburg: Herder, 1964).

[5]For the scriptural background of the term dogma see especially the article "dogma" in ThWNT II, 233-235 (Kittel). Cf. HthG, I, 225 (Geiselmann) and RAC, III, 1258 (Ranft).

[6]Kasper, Dogma unter dem Wort Gottes, 29-30.

employed in particular at Christian baptism.[7] Such creedal

formulae are distinguished from the Vatican understanding of

dogma in a number of ways. The most apparent distinction is

that they, like the statements of the early councils up to

Chalcedon, retained the form of doxology or confession and

were not directed at the precise propositional statement of

belief and identification of error. Edmund Schlink has

observed that this same doxological pattern is more charac-

teristic of the confessions of the pre-Chalcedonian councils

than it is of the formulations of Chalcedon itself and of

subsequent councils. The normal linguistic introduction to

such confessions is the "we believe" of Nicea. At Chalcedon,

the formula became "We teach, that it ought to be confessed,"

and the purpose of dogmatic definitions became less doxologi-

cal and more concerned with the precise delimitation of orth-

odox Church teaching.[8] As is well known, Adolf Harnack viewed

---

[7]Heinrich Schlier has noted the points of similarity between such creedal formulations and the modern Catholic understanding of dogma. "Kerygma und Sophia. Zur neutestamentlichen Grundlegung des Dogmas," in Die Zeit der Kirche
(Freiburg: Herder, 1957), pp. 226-232. Cf. similar observations in Rahner-Lehmann, Kerygma and Dogma, 50-55 and in
Peter Lengsfeld, Überlieferung und Schrift, 62. See also
H. Conzelmann, "Zur Analyse der Bekenntnisformel, I. Kor.
15:3-5," EvT 25 (1965), 1-15.

[8]DS 150 (credo); DS 125 (credimus). Contrast DS 301
(...confiteri...docemus). For an analysis of the shift, see
E. Schlink, "Die Struktur der dogmatischen Aussage als Oekumenisches Problem," 266. Schlink summarizes the development
in this way: "...die Eingangsworte machen deutlich dass es
sich hier nicht mehr um das gottesdienstliche Bekenntnis
selbst, sondern um die Lehre vom rechten Bekenntnis handelt."
The "anathema" form accompanied this structural change. "Mit
dieser Verschiebung aber tritt nicht nur der doxologische

68

this change in attitudes and the impact of Greek philosophy which it implied as a distortion of the Christian message. Few Protestant theologians would accept this extreme diagnosis today. This does not, however, prevent the recognition of the creative insights of pre-Chalcedonian tradition and thus a reemphasis of the points of continuity between dogma and kerygma and doxology and definition inadequately preserved in the theoretical and philosophical turn of the fourth century. Such a reemphasis will be investigated more fully at a later point in this study.

The medieval concept of dogma also differs in some apparent ways from the Vatican definition. As A. Lang has shown, "dogma" was not the preferred form of expression in the Middle Ages.[9] Articulus fidei was the more common usage. The points of difference between such articuli and the Vatican notion of dogma are informative. The articles of faith were not solely propositional expressions of the objective content of belief which compelled the assent of faith. The subjective appropriation of the content of faith, the fides qua, was of equal if not greater importance than the content of belief, the fides quod. As Walter Kasper has pointed out, "Medieval theology at least up to the Council of Trent,

---

sondern auch der positiven Zeugnischarakter des Bekenntnisses zurück; an die Stelle des Zeugnisses vor der Welt tritt die Abgrenzung von der Welt." (266). For a similar interpretation see RGG, II, 221 (Gloege).

[9]A. Lang, "Der Bedeutungswandel der Begriffe 'fides' und 'haeresis,'" 133-146.

measured the area of 'belief' by the extent of the inner commitment to a total moral and religious claim."[10] Thus the terms "faith" and "heresy" referred not so much to the propositional "accuracy" of expressions of faith, as to the inner attitude of belief--the obedience and commitment or the opposition to the Christian gospel.[11] With this understanding of faith, the propositional statements of belief in the form of the articuli fidei received a distinctive focus. The articles were measured not merely by their objective content, but by their soteriological efficacy: "Articulus est perceptio divinae veritatis tendens in ipsam."[12] Individual articles were not viewed in isolation from one another but in relationship to all the other articles of faith and to the saving reality which came to expression in them.[13] The meaning of articles of faith was thus

---

[10] Kasper, Dogma unter dem Wort Gottes, 30. Cf. L. Hödl, "Articulus Fidei," in Einsicht und Glaube. Festschrift für G. Söhngen (Freiburg: Herder, 1963), pp. 358-376.

[11] Kasper, Dogma unter dem Wort Gottes, 38-41. Cf. A. Lang, "Der Bedeutungswandel der Begriffe 'fides' und 'haeresis,'" whose historical study forms the basis of Kasper's own opinion. A similar conclusion based on a historical study of the term "fides" may be found in Piet Fransen, "The Authority of Councils," in Problems of Authority, ed. by John Todd (Baltimore: Helicon, 1962), pp. 72-74. Fransen has also touched on this point in "Reflexions sur l'anathème au concile de Trente," ETL 29 (1953), 657-672.

[12] St. Thomas Aquinas, Summa Theologiae, II, II, q. 1, a. 6.

[13] A. Hödl, "Articulus Fidei," 374.

closely linked to their existential relevance, their ability
to communicate the saving message of Christianity and direct
man to his ultimate beatific vision. Subjective acceptance
and understanding and not some timeless, abstract content
was essential. By a concern for the existential and not
merely the formal and rational truth of dogma, and by a
concern for the unity of all the articles of faith, medieval
theology adopted a much broader perspective of dogma than
that found in post-Tridentine tradition and at Vatican I.

The history of the concept of dogma up to and including
the Middle Ages did not produce a definition like that of
the first Vatican Council. The use of the term in the Vatican sense--a truth of revelation formally defined as such by
the Church--is a product of the Catholic theology of the
eighteenth and nineteenth centuries. In their careful historical studies of the history of the term "dogma," A.
Deneffe and Walter Kasper have located the first description
of dogma embodying both elements of the Vatican definition
in the writings of Philip Neri Chrismann (1751-1840). In his
Regula fidei catholicae (1792), Chrismann states: "A dogma
of the faith is nothing other than a divinely revealed doctrine and truth, which is proposed in a public judgment of
the Church as something to be believed by divine faith, in
such a way that the contrary is condemned by the Church as a
heretical doctrine."[14] Not only a formal decision but a

---

[14] A. Deneffe: "Dogma. Wort und Begriff," 538. Kasper

teaching universally accepted in the Church was included by
Chrismann in the category of such "public" judgments.
Chrismann's narrow definition of dogma was viewed at the
time as too minimalistic, and his book was placed on the In-
dex in 1869. Yet, surprisingly, his understanding of dogma
was generally accepted in nineteenth century theology and by
Vatican I. Chrismann's emphasis on the conceptual clarity
and formal authority of dogma reflects the background of post-
Tridentine theology discussed in the first chapter. After
the Council of Trent, dogma was interpreted in increasingly
juridical and rationalist terms. In the polemical response
to the attacks of Reformation, Humanism, and historical criticism, and later in the response to rationalist and modernist movements within the Church, attention turned away from
the "inner" authority of dogmatic statements, their ability
to express the loosely defined saving mystery of faith, to
a concern for conceptual precision and "outer" juridical
authority. Dogma achieved its contemporary form and over-
whelming importance to faith as a product of the growing
separation of Catholic thought from the historical and hermeneutical currents of the modern age. When placed in the
context of this historical background and when juxtaposed to
the broader concepts of dogma in earlier Catholic tradition,

_____

Dogma unter dem Wort Gottes, 35ff. The Latin text quoted in
Kasper reads: "Quod dogma fidei nil aliud sit, quam doctrina
et veritas divinitus revelata, quae publico Ecclesiae iudicio
fide divina credenda ita proponitur, ut contraria ab Ecclesiae tamquam haeretica doctrina damnetur." For Chrismann's
influence on the Roman School, see Kasper, Die Lehre von der
Tradition, 202.

the narrowness of the modern definition can be more fully appreciated. The new openness of Catholic theology to history and hermeneutic, as well as the reappropriation of the insights of earlier theology, point to the possibility of a reformulation of the concept of dogma, and, as remains to be seen, of the process of its interpretation. The precise direction of such a reformulation can be more adequately indicated, however, only after a closer examination of the Vatican definition itself.

III. The Definition of Dogma by the Church

The preliminary problem in the hermeneutic of dogma is locating those texts which have the status of dogma. How is dogma identified? The answer of Vatican I to this question was that dogmas of faith are formally proposed as truths of revelation by the magisterium of the Church, normally by the "solemn judgment" of a council or through a pope speaking ex cathedra. A full treatment of this understanding of the definition of dogma would necessitate an investigation of the notion of authority in the Church and especially the authority of the hierarchical magisterium. As this full treatment is beyond the scope of this study, only those aspects of the authority question which have the most direct impact on the hermeneutical problem will be considered. Central among these is the notion of "formal" authority. It is the formal authority of the magisterium, as we have already seen, that is for Ebeling the primary avenue of the Catholic escape from the hermeneutical problem.

A notion of formal authority, as Karl Rahner has pointed
out, is not a recent development in the Catholic Church. By
the end of the apostolic period, two elements of "authority"
were clearly affirmed in Catholic faith: 1) A material ele-
ment--the content of faith itself normatively expressed in
the teaching of the apostles; 2) A formal element--the claim
of the bishops, by reason of apostolic succession, to demand
faith as they testified in the name of Christ and with the
assistance of the Holy Spirit.[15] Before the twelfth century,
the focus of theology was on the first of these two themes--
the "material" authority of the mystery of faith or Christ-
event. After the Gregorian reform, however, as was indicated
in the first chapter, the attention of theology shifted to
the problem of formal-juridicial authority in the Church and
particularly to that of the hierarchy. With the challenge
of the Reformers, this emphasis was intensified and came to
dominate post-Tridentine theology. It is not surprising that,
in the authority conscious decades of the nineteenth century,
this same concern with extrinsic authority dominated the
theological scene and the decrees of Vatican I.[16] One of the
primary contributions of Vatican II was to present an image
of the Church less dependent on juridical categories. The

---

[15] Karl Rahner, "Magisterium," Sacramentum Mundi, III, 351.

[16] For a survey of the historical change in the notion of
authority see Yves Congar, "The Historical Development of
Authority in the Church. Points for Christian Reflection,"
in John Todd, Problems of Authority, 119-151.

theology of this century is marked by a similar reassertion of "intrinsic" or "material" authority in the Church. Little is to be gained today from purely formal claims of an office or title. Authority must convince, demonstrate a technical competence, and communicate meaning rather than merely demand automatic assent. It is even more clear following the controversies over Humanae Vitae that authority can no longer rely merely on formal claims to produce the assent of faith. Such a transformed understanding of authority has had a clear impact on the teaching of the "ordinary" magisterium.[17] The impact on the teaching of the "extraordinary" magisterium and thus on dogma is, however, less apparent. What the authority of dogma might be in this modern era and the implications of this authority for the hermeneutic of dogma remain to be explored.

In the first place, some strictly mechanical difficulties surround the notion of dogmatic definition. What is a formal definition? The question has been answered in various ways, but the usual response is that dogma is the product of an explicit definition by a general or ecumenical council or by a pope speaking ex cathedra. This seemingly clear criterion for distinguishing dogma conceals some ambiguities. Hubert Jedin, for example, has pointed out the difficulties inherent

---

[17]The teaching authority of the ordinary magisterium is treated by B. Schüller, "Bemerkungen zur authentischen Verkündigung des kirchlichen Lehramtes," Theologie und Philosophie 42 (1967), 534-551. Schüller points out that authority can no longer rest on merely formal claims; the best test of real authority is its effectiveness.

in the attempt to identify general or ecumenical councils; the canonical prerequisites of papal convocation, etc. simply do not apply to particular important councils in the history of the Church. Disputes over the ecumenical status of the Council of Constance and thus the dogmatic weight of its conciliarist decrees points to the problem that surrounds the formal identification of dogma.[18] Another source of difficulty is that dogma has not been limited to such explicit definitions by pope or council. Coupled to these "extraordinary" or explicit definitions has been a widespread recognition, following the teaching of Vatican I, of the dogmatic character of teaching of the "ordinary and universal" magisterium.[19] There is an obvious difficulty in identifying such universal teaching. In his recent study of papal infallibility, Hans Küng has argued that the teaching on contraception in the early part of the twentieth century fits in the category of such teaching and thus enjoys a claim

----

[18]A defense of the ecumenical status of the Council of Constance may be found in Hans Küng, Structures of the Church (Notre Dame: U. of Notre Dame, 1964), pp. 240ff.

[19]Two different realities should not be confused: 1) the "ordinary and universal" magisterium which, following the teaching of Vatican I, makes a claim to infallibility; 2) the "ordinary" (but not universal), "merely authentic" magisterium (papal encyclicals, pastoral letters, etc.) which makes no claim to infallibility. The teaching included by Vatican I as one form of dogma were those formulae taught universally in the Church as revealed truth. For two recent affirmations of the infallibility of the universal teaching of the ordinary magisterium, in this qualified sense, see Rahner-Lehmann, Kerygma and Dogma, 37-38 and Magnus Lohrer, Mysterium Salutis, I, 573.

to "formal" infallibility.[20] His interpretation has been
disputed by a number of theologians who believe Küng has
extended the scope of infallibility too far in this instance; the teaching on birth control, they maintain, was
never universally taught as revealed truth.[21] Even if one
rejects Küng's contention that the traditional teaching on
birth control is "formally" infallible, however, the debate
indicates that sufficient unclarity surrounds the identifying "marks" of dogma to make possible differences of opinion
as to which teachings enjoy dogmatic status. No definitive
accepted list of the dogmas has been or can be drawn up;
hard and fast divisions between dogma and other Church teaching are impossible.

The formal identification of dogma is much less a rigid
demarcation of fallible from infallible teaching than it is
an indication of the general importance assigned in Catholic
faith to expressions of the belief of the Church as a whole.
The continuity and truth of Catholic faith is not grounded
solely in the interpretative acumen of the autonomous indi-
dual, but in the consensus of the Church, both in the past
and in the present. Interpretations of Scripture and of
doctrinal expressions of faith properly occur in and with the
Church in order to provide a foundation for a common faith

---

[20]Hans Küng, Infallibility? An Inquiry (New York:
Doubleday, 1971), pp. 51ff.

[21]For such a criticism see Richard P. Mcbrien, The Infallibility Debate, ed. by John J. Kirven (New York: Paulist,
1971), p. 45 and footnote #15.

and visible Church unity. This is not to say that dogmatic
definitions are the normal or even the most important means
of transmitting faith and of guaranteeing its unity. Preaching, liturgy, Christian education, the teaching of the ordinary magisterium, and the everyday life of the Christian
community are of greater importance. Crisis situations have
arisen in the history of the Church, however, when a clear
statement of belief and identification of error were required.
It is not impossible that such situations may arise again in
the future. Moreover, some of these ecclesial decisions of
the past, e.g., the christological and trinitarian definitions of the early councils, have assumed places of central
importance in Christian faith. The community sense of faith
has in fact taken the form of accepted and binding expressions of belief. To recognize the formal authority of such
ecclesial expressions is to accept them as qualitatively more
important sources for reflection and theological interpretation than the statements of individual theologians. They provide unifying points for theological reflection, for Church
teaching, and for proclamation and have necessarily a certain
"binding" quality. The presupposition guiding interpretation
of dogmatic statements is of their truth rather than of their
falsity--of their importance to faith rather than of their
irrelevance.

In the context of eighteenth and nineteenth century positivistic hermeneutic, such presuppositions would have seemed
too biased and too grounded in tradition and thus contrary to

the critical and objective determination of truth. A key
aspect of the contemporary hermeneutical discussion, however,
and particularly of the hermeneutical theory of Hans-Georg
Gadamer, is a renewed appreciation of the importance of dogmatic consciousness.[22] All interpretation begins with presuppositions, with a "preunderstanding." The ideal of presuppositionless interpretation contradicts the basic structure of understanding in the human sciences. Tradition is
not necessarily inimical to but rather a guide to truth. In
remembrance of the past, the historical continuity supplied
by tradition forms the preunderstanding of the interpreter
and is the basis of understanding. Particularly in the interpretation of essential dogmatic assertions, the interpreter does not start from scratch--his mind is not a blank
slate waiting to be filled in. Historical understanding, to
borrow Gadamer's descriptive terms, is a "fusion" of the
horizon of the interpreter, including his dogmatic preunderstanding, and the "horizon" of the past dogmatic text. To
recognize the authority of dogmatic tradition, therefore, is
simply to take account of one of the key features of human
historicality and of the historical path to truth. The "formal" authority of dogma is twofold: it entails an idea of
those historical texts of importance to faith, and it includes
possible preunderstandings of given meanings of traditional
texts which become part of the act of understanding.

---

[22] See Gadamer, Wahrheit und Methode. Grundzüge einer
philosophischen Hermeneutik (Tübingen: J. C. B. Mohr, 1960),
esp. pp. 261ff. The importance of Gadamer's work in this
study will become apparent.

To assert the importance of dogma as a "source" for theology and even to note the possibility of preunderstood meanings is not, however, to come to terms with the key hermeneutical problem. The Catholic notion of the authority of dogma does not present a "solution" to the hermeneutical question, as Ebeling maintains. A recognition of the authority of dogma, even of the formal impossibility of contradicting dogma, does not solve the problem of interpreting particular dogmatic texts. A need to identify the meaning of dogma points to the necessity of moving between the historical situation of the text and the situation of interpretation. A recognition of the importance of a continuing remembrance of dogmatic tradition in Catholic faith and theology does not provide a "special" hermeneutic which escapes the tensions of history and resolves the hermeneutic problem. Stated concisely, the formal authority of dogma and its claim to express infallible truth have little actual importance unless they affect the hermeneutical process. Dogma must have meaning to bind authoritatively or to communicate truth. Given this state of affairs, it is not surprising that a Catholic emphasis on the authority and truth of dogma was coupled in the classical phase of Catholic theology with a number of theories of interpretation. Before examining these, however, let us look at the second main element of the Vatican definition--the identification of dogma as "revealed" truth.

IV.   Dogma as "Revealed" Truth

The second feature of dogma noted by Vatican I is that it expresses a truth of revelation and thus stands in continuity with Scripture. But what is meant by revelation? Catholic fundamental theology at the end of the last century and the beginning of the twentieth century stressed a noetic concept of revelation: that which is communicated to man in revelation is a "complex of truths necessary for salvation."[23] The dominant concept of revelation reflects the tradition of scholastic teaching which has defined revelation as "locutio dei attestans," or, in the concise description of Werner Bulst, "God speaking out of the treasury of his own understanding communicating to men truths which otherwise would be attainable by them only with difficulty or not at all."[24] A critique of this noetic or rationalist definition is a main theme of contemporary Catholic theology and needs no lengthy restatement.[25] The rationalist outlook deemphasizes the whole experiential framework of Christian revelation. It inadequately takes into account the givenness of revelation in historical deeds as well as in conceptual language, the role of the subjective faith response of the individual believer and of the faith community, the historicality of revelation in its

---

[23] This is Réné Latourelle's formulation of the teaching in Catholic fundamental theology. Theology of Revelation (New York: Alba, 1966), p. 204.

[24] Bulst, Revelation (New York: Herder, 1965), p. 17.

[25] See the critiques of Latourelle and Bulst as well as Gabriel Moran, Theology of Revelation (New York: Herder, 1966).

textual sources as well as in the "hearing" community of believers. Above all, a purely propositional notion of revelation only with difficulty grasps the movement of Christian tradition as the continuing _event_ of the personal encounter with Christ, rather than as the handing on of a static deposit of propositional truths.

When "revelation" is interpreted in its full experiential and historical context, the definition of dogma as "revealed" truth raises a number of concrete problems. How is dogma related to other expressions revelation in the faith community and thus to preaching, sacraments, etc.? Such a question becomes appropriate when revelation is no longer completely identified with the transmission of conceptual truths. If the subjective faith response of the believer, one involving the impact of revelation upon his own self-understanding, sense of identity, and sense of reality, is an essential element in the event of revelation, how does this personal dimension function in the "assent" to dogma? Specifically, this question may take the form of the conflict of individual conscience and the "binding" authority of dogmatic statements. All of these and other questions have been prompted by the movement away from a propositional notion of revelation and are part of a much broader effort to reinterpret the "presence" of revelation in Scripture and tradition along non-rationalist lines.

The basic themes of the Scripture-tradition controversy within Catholic thought have reflected a propositional understanding of revelation. Discussions of the "sufficiency" of Scripture, or the independent status of tradition as a "source" of revelation, as well as the whole problematic of doctrinal development have been closely tied to a propositional revelation. They have presumed a specific "content" of revelation, propositionally expressible, which must be located in Scripture and/or in the tradition of the Church. A non-propositional understanding of revelation has brought a change in this approach to the tradition problem which is concisely described by Josef Ratzinger:

> The comprehensive problem of the mode of presence of the revealed word among the faithful must be dealt with as a whole. Then it becomes clear that we must go behind the positive sources, scripture and tradition, to their inner source, revelation, the living word of God, from which scripture and tradition spring and without which their significance for faith cannot be understood. The question of scripture and tradition remains insoluble as long as it is not expanded into a question of revelation and tradition and thus inserted into the larger context to which it belongs.[26]

Scripture and tradition are properly examined as witnesses to a revelation which they express but which is not identified with them. Dogmas, other texts of tradition, and the text of Scripture itself stand under the word of God. They point beyond themselves to the reality of revelation which they make known but do not simply replace. Such a position is obviously not strikingly new; the consistent tradition in the Catholic Church has not been a simple identification of

---

[26]Josef Ratzinger, Revelation and Tradition (New York: Herder, 1970), pp. 34-35.

Scripture and tradition with the Gospel.[27] As was suggested
in the first chapter, however, the theoretical separation of
Scripture, tradition, and word of God has been coupled to a
practical inability to maintain the distinction. What is
new in the contemporary Catholic approach to the Scripture-
tradition problem is the desire to preserve the critical
freedom of the word of God over Scripture and tradition, and
to do so by grounding this critical freedom in an adequate
hermeneutic. A reformulation of the propositional understanding of revelation has, in effect, been accompanied by a reformulation of the Scripture-tradition problem in hermeneutical terms. What hermeneutic will assist the movement from
Scripture and tradition to the expression of the saving message of Christianity in the changing historical situation of
faith? Dogma, in particular, has emerged as a hermeneutical
problem in the last two centuries because it has seemed to
be more a block than an aid to such a movement. The formal
claim to revealed truth has done little to enhance the concrete effectiveness of dogma as an expression of the renewing
power of the word of God. Edmund Schlink has observed that
Christians have found it possible to pray together, to study
the bible and worship together. Ecumenical dialogue has been
frustrated, however, the moment the discussion has turned to

---

[27]See, for example, Congar's summary of the history of
the concept of "gospel" in the Catholic Church, TT, 281, 158-
160. Cf. Kasper, Dogma unter dem Wort Gottes, 84-90. Vatican I pointed to a similar understanding, although in intellec-
tualist terms, in its distinction of the depositum fidei from
its expression in dogma. Kasper, ibid., 45; cf. Rahner-
Lehmann, Kerygma and Dogma, 10.

dogma.[28] Such a phenomenon is curiously out of harmony with the reconciling function of the gospel. Renewal within the Catholic Church has also seemed to be more frustrated than assisted by dogmatic teaching. Too often dogma has seemed to hold the Church in the past and render it incapable of finding the new options necessary for the movement into the future.[29] Both phenomena support Harnack's conclusion that dogma and gospel stand not in unity but in irreconcilable tension.

Still another dimension of the problem of dogma has been its effect on the dialogue of Church and world. Since the Enlightenment, dogma has appeared to modern man as a flight into abstraction and illusion and away from the real world of experience. Acceptance of dogma has seemed, in the Enlightenment pattern of thought, to involve an abdication of critical reason by the individual and blind obedience to formal teaching authority. Dogmatic beliefs seem to be closed to the process of correction and revision that characterizes other areas of belief. Such criticism is appropriate in light of some forms of dogmatic theology and belief, both Catholic and Protestant. But the flat rejection of tradition overlooks the positive significance of tradition as an avenue to truth, just as it overlooks the necessary function in understanding of presuppositions formed in the interpreter by the

---

[28]E. Schlink, "Die Struktur der dogmatischen Aussage," 251.

[29]Kasper, Dogma unter dem Wort Gottes, 7.

tradition in which he stands. We will return to this point
in the discussion of the hermeneutical function of a "dogmatic" preunderstanding. It should be noted at this point,
however, that the Enlightenment critique and other factors
combined to undermine the continuity of dogma and revelation
or gospel. As Walter Kasper has observed, the problem touches
not this or that dogma, but the notion of dogma itself. The
question is the nature of dogma. Can it be an expression of
the word of God in the modern age?[30]

     The reformulation of the Scripture-tradition problem
and of the nature of revelation described here in an admittedly cursory fashion have counteracted any attempt to simply
identify dogma with the gospel. Defined as a truth of revelation in the proper sense, dogma is "revelation" to the
extent that it acts on experience and stands in unity with
the saving proclamation of Christianity. Only by ever-renewed
interpretation does dogma express the living word of God in
any particular age. It is an event in understanding and not
a static possession or law. At the same time, however, it
has become impossible to separate the gospel from the process
of tradition, including its dogmatic forms. A growing awareness of the historicality of Scripture in particular has
demonstrated the complexity of traditions in the bible itself
and has pointed out the illusion of any simple opposition of
kerygma and tradition, dogma and gospel. A close continuity

---

[30]Kasper, Dogma unter dem Wort Gottes, 12.

of "dogmatic" forms of tradition and the Christian kerygma
has been demonstrated to be a part of Scripture itself.[31]
Fixed confessions of faith in the biblical writings (e.g.,
I. Cor. 15:3-5; Rom. 1:3f.; I Thes. 1:9-10) point to the
importance of creedal formulae as coordinating points for
the gospel even in the apostolic period. Doctrine and gospel
are linked in the earliest stage of Church history without
being simply identified with one another. The question of
the dialectical unity of the two thus emerged in the early
years of Christianity and has received no definitive resolution from then down to the present day.[32] What hermeneutic will permit dogma to become "revelation"--an expression
of the meaning of Christian faith in an existential sense?
As in the case of the authority of dogma, the assertion
that dogma expresses a truth of revelation raises but does
not resolve the hermeneutical problem.

---

[31]See footnote #4 of this chapter.

[32]Kasper has stated the contemporary form of the problem
in this way. "Als erstes Ergebnis der gegenwärtigen theologischen Diskussion können wir festhalten: Die alte liberale
Gegenüberstellung von Evangelium und Dogma ist heute unmöglich
geworden, da das Evangelium keine vom dogmatischen Traditionsprozess historisch ablösbare Grösse darstellt. Diesem ersten
Ergebnis ist aber sofort ein zweites hinzuzufügen: Ebensowe-
nig wie das Evangelium vom Traditionsprozess historisch
ablösbar ist, ist es dogmatisch mit diesem identisch. Das
Evangelium ist vielmehr die Macht des erhöhten Herrn in und
über der Kirche durch sein lebendiges Wort...eine gegenwärtige
Macht, die sich in Bekenntnis und Zeugnis der Kirche immer
neu Ausdruck verschafft, ohne jemals in diesem Bekenntnis
aufzugehen." Dogma unter dem Wort Gottes, 23-24.

V. The Hermeneutic of Dogma: Some Classical Approaches

The changed understanding of the authority of dogma and
of its character as "revealed" truth points to one clear conclusion. Both the authority and truth of dogma are inextricably bound to the determination of meaning. The meaning of
dogma, like that of Scripture, emerges in the movement between historical texts and the present situation of faith.
A recognition of the full historicality of dogmatic statements
carries with it the need to "translate" the meaning of authoritative texts from one historical situation to another in a
way which preserves their significance and importance for
Christian faith. This translation is subject to the same
structures of historicality that are involved in the interpretation of scripture and thus to the hermeneutical problem.
Our concern now is to examine some of the main approaches to
the interpretation of dogma which have neglected, as Ebeling
claims, the historicality of dogmatic statements and the full
implications of the hermeneutical problem, and then to note
the new awareness of the historicality of dogma in contemporary Catholic thought.

A. The "Clarity" of Dogma

At first glance, the problem of interpretation seems to
be less apparent in the case of dogma than in the case of
Scripture. For the most part, dogmatic definitions are in
Latin and are part of a long history of theological reflection
in the Latin language. Over the centuries, many Latin theological terms employed in dogma have been honed to a concep-

tual precision that is missing in the case of biblical language. This linguistic and theological unity can make the point of a dogmatic text "clearer" than the historically more complex and elusive meanings of Scripture. By its very nature, a dogmatic definition often enjoys a clarity and conceptual precision not found in the less reflective articulations of the biblical authors. Moreover, dogmatic texts can be more easily abstracted from their given historical situations--from the conjunction of a particular author and a particular audience. "Definitions" by nature are attempts to articulate basic principles of Christian faith in a precise and clear form. Thus while the concrete <u>Sitz-im-Leben</u> of a scriptural text is often intrinsically connected to the text's meaning, dogma can appeal to a universality of meaning less bound to given historical contexts. These and other hermeneutical "advantages" in part account for the near absence of a Catholic discussion of the hermeneutic of dogma. Particularly after Vatican I, Catholic theologians seized the "stability" of meaning that dogma seems to enjoy as a means of responding to the modernists and to the challenges of historical criticism.[33]

Such appeals to the "clarity" of dogma, although they contain an element of truth, provide no solution to the hermeneutical problem. What they overlook is the full scope

---

[33]Piet Fransen, "Einige Bemerkungen zu den theologischen Qualifikationen," in <u>Die Interpretation des Dogmas</u>, ed. by Piet Schoonenberg, 113.

of the <u>historical</u> <u>problem</u> of locating the meaning of dogma.
The various aspects of this problem will be analyzed in the
next two chapters, but some main features of the problem can
be noted to indicate that the clear and univocal meanings of
dogmatic statements often become clouded with an insight into
history. In the first place, despite the fact that Latin is
now a "dead" language, Latin words, like those of any other
language, are rooted in concrete historical contexts. Latin
theological terms have in fact changed meanings as they moved
through history. New historical situations, new theological
questions have expanded the meaning of concepts often to the
point of contradicting earlier tradition.[34] A long theological tradition of interpretation may be more a barrier than an
aid to reaching the original sense of a definition. To begin
interpretation of dogmatic texts with the assumption that the
meaning of key terms is clear is simply to overlook the ambi-

---

[34]See, e.g., the study of the change in the meanings of
the terms <u>fides</u> and <u>haeresis</u> by A. Lang (footnote #6) and the
similar reflections of P. Fransen in "The Authority of Councils,"
pp. 72-74. Fransen concludes his study of this process of historical change in this way: "When we show the need and duty of
making a previous study of the historical sense of conciliar
definitions, we meet with a very common objection. Why should
theologians be forced to engage in studies which are often very
difficult and yet completely useless, since the 'obvious sense'
of a text ought to be amply sufficient for the correct reading
of a conciliar text. What is forgotten is that there is nothing less certain than the 'obvious sense' of a text. Psychol-
ogy, philosophy, classical and modern logic as well as modern
linguistic analysis abundantly demonstrate what experience
teaches, namely, that the sense of a word is always and necessarily determined <u>by</u> <u>its</u> <u>context</u>."

guity that can affect dogmatic language. The seeming clarity
of meaning of a dogma also often dissolves when a deeper look
is taken at the historical circumstances surrounding the originally intended meaning. The meaning of dogma rests in the
complex interrelationship of the conscious intentions of those
formulating a dogma, assuming these can be found, and the
implicit dimensions of meaning included in the horizon of the
authors and involved in a given text. The determination of
these meanings can carry the interpreter through a consideration of the text, the acts of a given council, and the historical and cultural milieu influencing a given definition.
Finally, particular dogmatic statements are properly located
in relationship to the basic subject matter of Christian faith
and thus considered in light of Scripture and tradition as a
whole, including other dogmatic definitions and key aspects
of the Christian message not formally defined. At all of
these levels of meaning, the "clarity" of dogma may dissolve
under investigation.[35]

To have taken account of the original sense of a definition and of the tradition in which a definition stands is not

---

[35]For similar observations of the need to take account of
the historicality of dogmatic language see G. C. Berkouwer,
The Second Vatican Council and the New Catholicism (Grand
Rapids: Eerdmans, 1965), p. 78 and M. Lohrer, "Überlegungen
zur Interpretation lehramtlicher Aussagen als Frage des Ökumenischen Gesprächs," in Gott in Welt. Festgabe für Karl
Rahner, vol. II, (Freiburg: Herder, 1964), p. 349. Löhrer
puts the problem in this form: "Wird eine Interpretations-
bedürftigketi der Schrift aus ihrem Buch-Charakter abgeleitet,
so ist das Lehramt in seinen früheren geschribenen Äusserungen
nicht wenige interpretationsbedürftig."

enough. Such past meanings must still be translated into the present situation of faith. When the meaning of dogma is sought, and not merely its abstract authority or truth claim, then this mediation of past texts into the present is demanded. Both Scripture and doctrinal tradition are "remembered" and "handed on" to the extent that they are shown to stand in continuity with the concrete experience of reality in any given historical epoch.[36] Locating the "clear" original meaning of a definition may still fall short of this type of understanding. As Edward Schillebeeckx has observed, "Anyone who maintains--as some do--that Trent, because it is formulating a dogma is, in what it explicitly says (das Gesagte), a priori an answer to my present day questions is radically misconceiving the historicality of man's existence, of human questioning and of all human questioning and of all human understanding."[37] A point of contact with the questions of modern man and thus with real and not hypothetical needs and concerns is an intrinsic element of authentic historical understanding. As has already been noted, it is precisely this continuity of dogma and experience which today is very difficult to maintain. The starting point of a consideration of the

---

[36]Ernst Fuchs has pointed out that dogmatic teaching, like Scripture, may stand in tension with contemporary experience, and, in such instances, neither the truth nor normativeness of dogma will be self-evident. Marburger Hermeneutik (Tübingen: J. C. B. Mohr, 1968), p. 33.

[37]Edward Schillebeeckx, "Towards a Catholic Use of Hermeneutics," 11.

hermeneutical problem of dogma is the recognition that dogma is more often a block than an aid to faith in the modern period. This crisis of meaning affects not only secondary or peripheral affirmations--such as the teaching on indulgences, now easily seen to be a relic of the past. The crisis extends as well to central concerns of faith--to the problems of God and of Christology, just to name two examples. To raise the question of the "meaning" of these central dogmatic affirmations, now and in Christian tradition, is to ask in a real way about the communication and survival of faith in the contemporary age. Stated concisely, the hermeneutic of dogma entails consideration of the full historicality of a dogmatic text and of the process of interpretation. A more careful examination of historicality and the hermeneutical problem remain to be carried out, as well as the attempt to relate this discussion to the hermeneutic of dogma. Our object up to this point has been to show that the presupposition of the "clarity" of dogma collapses with the recognition of the historicality of dogmatic texts and the historicality of interpretation.

B. The Appeal to Authority

What one might call the _claritas dogmatis_ has been further secured, especially in post-Vatican I theology, by an appeal to the interpretative authority of the magisterium. The Council of Trent established the principle that the magisterium is the normative judge and interpreter of the Word of God

and thus of Sacred Scripture.[38] This principle has been extended in the location of the magisterium as the normative
interpreter of dogma. In its original Tridentine formulation,
the responsibility assigned to the magisterium to judge the
true sense of Scripture did not simply hand over the task of
interpretation to the hierarchy. Rather, the magisterium was
to select from and judge the truth of already existing interpretations supplied by the doctores and teachers of the
Church.[39] A growing emphasis on authority after Trent brought,
however, a clear shift in emphasis. The magisterium became
increasingly the interpreter and not merely the judge of interpretation. This position, Max Seckler has pointed out, has
been affirmed by recent popes, especially by Pius XII and by
Paul VI.[40] Recent papal and theological teaching has main-
tained that the magisterium, by its claim of authority and
supported by the assistance of the Holy Spirit, supplies "clarity" where historical unclarity prevails. A number of related
affirmations have been made. If the magisterium expresses the
normative and clear sense of dogma and Scripture, then scholar-
ly opinions cannot be employed in criticism of the magisterium.

---

[38]DS, 1507. For a historical study of the background and
original sense of this definition see Hans Kümmeringer, "Es
ist Sache der Kirche, 'iudicare de vere sensu et interpretatione scriptuarum sanctarum,'" Theologische Quartelschrift 149
(1969), 282-296.

[39]Kümmeringer, "Es ist Sache," 294. Cf. Max Seckler, "Die
Theologie als kirchliche Wissenschaft nach Pius XII und Paul VI,"
Theologische Quartelschrift 149 (1969), 209-235.

[40]Seckler, "Die Theologie als kirchliche Wissenschaft,"
212-214. Contrast Lumen Gentium, #25 where the bond of the
magisterium to theology is affirmed clearly.

Further, because the teaching office is the normative interpreter, theology, although it may be of assistance in the
formulation and interpretation of definitions, cannot determine the final meaning of authoritative texts. The interpretative method enjoyed by the hierarchical magisterium rests
not on the competence of scholars but on the charism of the
Holy Spirit.[41] The "true" meaning of Scripture and tradition
can be isolated from the welter of conflicting opinions, and
this authoritatively guaranteed interpretation then binds lay-
men and theologian alike not merely in an external manner but
in the inner forum of conscience.[42] As in some classical
Catholic theories of tradition, hierarchical authority has
been seized as a response to the hermeneutical problem.

The solution to the hermeneutic problem by an appeal to
authority has been challenged in recent Catholic theology in
a number of ways. Above all, as has already been mentioned,
the notion of authority is in the process of reformulation.
Authority in the Church is now conceived in a "material" and
not merely in a "formal" light. Authoritative teaching must
rely on more than a formal claim to express the truth of any
given teaching. A competence of interpretation must be demonstrated, and, in the interpretation of dogma, a competent
determination of meaning can no more bypass the demands of

---

[41]Seckler, "Die Theologie als kirchliche Wissenschaft,"
220-223.

[42]Ibid., 224.

historical awareness than in the interpretation of Scripture.[43] This realization has undermined any magisterial claims to determine the meaning of traditional texts in a way free from the problems presented by historical awareness. It has also produced a very lively discussion of the freedom of theology and of its relationship to the magisterium.[44] If the historical pastness of dogmatic texts cannot be evaded, neither can the task of relating dogma to the present concerns of faith. An affirmation of the central "binding" truth of a definition not related to contemporary questions and experience overlooks an important aspect of historicality. Both an attentiveness to the demands of historical awareness and the need to translate dogma into the present situation of faith call in question the appeal to authority as a solution to the hermeneutical problem.

---

[43] Oswald Loretz maintains that we are now past the era when the magisterium could claim to determine the meaning of Scripture on its own. The sense of Scripture (and one might add of dogma) is only available through the normal method of historical interpretation. "Die hermeneutischen Grundsätze den Zweiten Vatikanischen Konzils," in Die hermeneutische Frage in der Theologie, ed. by Oswald Loretz and Walter Strolz (Freiburg: Herder, 1968), pp. 486ff.

[44] For examples of this discussion see Max Seckler, "Die Theologie als kirchliche Wissenschaft." See also Paul Touilleux, "Kritische Theologie," Theologische Quartelschrift 149 (1969), 235-259; Hermann Pottmeyer, "Kirchliche Lehrautorität und Wissenschaft--ein Gegensatz?" MüThZ 20 (1969), 85-103; and the articles in Paul Neuenzeit (ed.), Die Funktion der Theologie in Kirche und Gesellschaft (Munich, 1969).

C. The Form-Content Distinction

The most common approach to the interpretation of dogma in twentieth century Catholic theology has been the distinction of the unchanging "content" or "essence" of a dogmatic statement from its changing historical "form."[45] A definition is necessarily embodied in the language and thought forms of a particular historical epoch. Moreover, in its reappropriation through history, a dogma is reinterpreted and translated into different forms. The form-content distinction has been employed to isolate the "inner" meaning of dogmatic texts from this process of historical change. In its movement through history, a dogmatic statement is necessarily recast in different concepts and modes of expression, just as it was initially cast in the language and thought forms of a particular historical period. Within this historical development, however, the essential dogmatic affirmation remains the same. At the center of historical movement and flux is a stable, unchanging "content" of faith which is identical through the history of the Church although its expression may vary.

Such a form-content distinction allows some weight to be placed on the historical circumstances surrounding a definition. The "form" of a dogma is a partial, historically conditioned effort to express the real content of Christian faith.

---

[45]For an example of such an appeal to the distinction see Edward Schillebeeckx, Revelation and Theology, vol. I (New York: Sheed and Ward, 1967), p. 256. See also Michael Schmaus, Preaching as the Sacrament of the Encounter with God (Staten Island, N. Y.: Alba House, 1966), pp. 130-134.

As such, its historicality may be taken with full seriousness. The changeable and transitory status of the "form" of a defini- tion poses no real threat to the central meaning of dogma. The real content or meaning remains the same even though the formu- lation of the content changes. It is the content of dogma, as Michael Schmaus has emphasized, which is given by God. The inner affirmation is the revealed truth. The outer historical garb is supplied by theology and by the believing community and is subject to change.[46] This inner content is sometimes identified with a "common sense" meaning easily apprehended by all believers.[47] Such a basic, easily understood meaning seems to be necessary in the propositional approach to revelation, if the less intelligent are not to be made less capable of understanding those truths necessary for their salvation.[48] Even though precise philosophical categories may be employed in a definition, therefore, the "meaning" of dogma may not be tied to any philosophical terms or systems. A general, easily accessible meaning, not philosophically precise, but explicit enough to defend the truth of faith against particular errors, is that "meaning" which is essential to dogmatic statements.[49] New forms of dogmatic content are both necessary and good, but a change in content would represent heresy.

---

[46] Schmaus, Preaching, 130.

[47] E. Dublanchy, "Dogme," DTC, IV, 1591.

[48] Ibid., 1577-1588.

[49] Ibid., 1577-1578.

A way of locating the "inner" meaning of dogma similar
to the form-content division is the separation of a "fuller"
sense of dogmatic texts from the literal or historical forms
in which this sensus plenior is cast. In the last few
decades, the sensus plenior has been especially popular among
some Catholic biblical exegetes as a way to account for dogmatic statements which somehow reflect the "same" truth as
Scripture and yet, on the surface, seem to be quite different.[50] What is defined in dogma--the inner content or mean-
ing--is a fuller, mystical sense not perceptible from the
standpoint of critical history but, nonetheless, "there" in
the dogmatic or scriptural text. The separation of the "fuller" from the historical sense of texts of the past is made
even more complete when the real organ for interpreting the
sensus plenior is identified with the sensus fidelium.
Giovanni Filograssi, M. Dominikus Koster, Carl Balic and other
theologians of the modern period have emphasized the intuitive,
non-reflective faith sense of the Christian community as the
real organ of tradition.[51] As in mystical approaches to tradi-

---

[50] Richard Boeckler, Der moderne römisch-katholische Traditionsbegriff, surveys the use of the sensus plenior distinction among theologians. For an example of the appeal to the
sensus plenior as a solution to the problem of doctrinal development see Leo Scheffczyk, "Die Auslegung der Schrift als dogmatische Aufgabe," MüThZ 15 (1964), 190-204. One of the key
efforts to employ the sensus plenior in biblical interpretation
is that of Raymond Brown, The Sensus Plenior of Sacred Scripture (Baltimore: St. Mary's, 1955). Cf. Jerome Biblical
Commentary (Englewood Cliffs: Prentice-Hall, 1968), pp. 615ff.

[51] Ibid., 136ff.

tion, the lived faith experience of the Church and the reflection of this faith sense in the magisterium become the real
sources for the transmission of the faith. The reappropriation of tradition by theology and by Church historians from a
historical perspective is deemphasized, and the real meaning
of dogma is located at an "inner" level not open to the
vision of the critical historian.

The form-content distinction received a strong push from
Catholic theologians in the first half of the twentieth century as a response to the "extrinsicist" approach to tradition
criticized by Blondel. A separation of form and content
called in question any simple identification of the content
of dogma with one conceptual container, particularly with the
conceptual forms of Thomistic thought popular among the
Neoscholastic theologians. An affirmation of the distinction
between form and content was an attempt to preserve the possibility of historical development. Understandably, the intel-
lectualist or extrinsicist spokesmen were upset by the devaluation of the conceptual forms of dogma. Garrigou-Lagrange,
for example, could see in the form-content division of the
"New Theology" only a rejuvenation of the Modernist heresy.[52]
A separation of the concepts and terms of a definition from
its "inner" meaning, as Garrigou-Lagrange saw it, could only
call in question the immutable truth of dogma. Only if the
conceptuality is itself immutable, may an unchanging inner

---

[52]Garrigou-Lagrange, "L'immutabilité du dogme selon le
concile du Vatican et le relativisme," Angelicum 26 (1949),
309-310.

content be affirmed.[53] Garrigou-Lagrange was concerned above
all to see in dogma not a time-conditioned expression of
Christian experience, but instead an immutable description of
reality itself. Dogma is a "map" of the fixed structures of
external truth and not merely an expression of the experience
of the Christian community. Its conformation with the reality
of things is the final guarantee of its truth.[54] The affirmation of Jesus Christ as the second person of the Trinity is
as much a "fact" as his death on the cross and thus not subject to historical change.[55] Admittedly, the language of
dogma may not be clearly and fully understood and thus demand
theological reflection and clarification. But over the course
of time a "purification" process can make clear the precise
conceptual truth of dogmatic statements. If there is any
development, it is in the understanding of the community and
not in the dogma itself, neither in its "form" nor in its
"content."

As a critique of such an unhistorical vision of dogma
the form-content distinction is understandable. As Piet
Fransen has observed, to bind faith to one linguistic expression, as Garrigou-Lagrange seems to do, is to bind it to a

---

[53]Garrigou-Lagrange, "L'immutabilité des vérités definies
et le surnaturel," Angelicum 26 (1949), 285-287.

[54]Garrigou-Lagrange, "L'immutabilité du dogme," 313.

[55]Garrigou-Lagrange, "L'immutabilité des vérités definies,"
292.

"law which kills."[56] Such a restriction limits faith to one
traditionally defined way of expression and thus chains it to
the past. The historicality of all language, including that
of dogma, is overlooked as is the historical gap between authoritative texts of tradition and the changing situation of
faith. Reappropriation, translation, the problems posed by
new historical contexts and questions--all are not assigned
their proper place in the essentialist approach to dogma.

As a defense of the possibility of reinterpretation of
dogma and of historical development, the form-content distinction served a useful purpose. As a constructive vision of
historicality and the hermeneutic problem, however, the scheme
is less satisfactory. Although proponents of the form-content
theory do not identify the unchanging inner content of dogma
with a particular conceptual form, the problem posed by hermeneutical and historical awareness is this: how is such an
inner kernel of meaning to be located? If the interpretation
of dogma is always from a particular historical situation, how
can a timeless or unchanging essence of faith be determined?
Can the linguistic form of a definition and its "inner" content be in fact distinguished? Edward Schillebeeckx, a theologian who has employed the form-content division in the past,
was pushed to an awareness of all of these questions by his
reflection on the hermeneutical problem. His response has
been to question the usefulness of the form-content schema.

---

[56]Fransen, "Einige Bemerkungen zu den theologischen Qualifikationen," in Die Interpretation des Dogmas, 126.

The "meaning" of dogma always emerges in a concrete act of understanding. The distinction between the "dogmatic essence" and its historical mode of expression is therefore "virtually meaningless and unmanageable precisely because this 'essence' is never given to us as a pure essence, but is always concealed in a historical mode of expression."[57] No "pure" content of faith is ever supplied which is not itself the product of a particular interpretation.

> If we then discard that mode in which the reality/of faith/ was worded we are left with a content; it is, however, no more the "pure content of faith" than the earlier one was, but is simply a faithful interpretation in the light of our present situation. This interpretation, not a "timeless essence," contains for us the "pure content of faith."[58]

Michael Schmaus has observed in a similar vein that the linguistic form is "not just a dress which the content puts on." The form and content of all dogmatic definitions stand in a unity--they are one indivisible whole.[59] Pure or necessary ideas cannot be isolated from the contingent flow of history, because in any given interpretation, form is supplied by the very act of understanding.

Quite similar criticisms may be found in recent theology of the sensus plenior notion.[60] Raymond Brown, one of the

---

[57]Schillebeeckx, "Towards a Catholic Use of Hermeneutics," 12.

[58]Ibid., 11-12.

[59]Schmaus, Dogma, vol. I (New York: Herder, 1968), p. 193.

[60]R. Lapointe, Les trois dimensions de l'hérmeneutique (Paris: Gabalda, 1967), pp. 32-42.presents a penetrating cri-

major proponents of the sensus plenior, has concluded that
the distinction has been of little practical importance in his
own exegetical work. In theory he could affirm the separation
of the fuller from the literal or historical meaning of Scripture, but his interpretation worked through the normal chan-
nels of historical understanding.[61] Much as Schillebeeckx
concluded that the inner content of dogma could not be isolated
from its historical form, so Brown found it impossible to
separate a "fuller" or "spiritual" sense from the historically
determined meanings of Scripture. An increasing recognition
of historicality has brought an unwillingness, indeed an
inability, to separate "historical" from "spiritual" meaning
and a new attentiveness to the hermeneutical problem. The
attempt of theologians to locate the "pure" or "spiritual" content of a dogmatic teaching founders, as did the claritas of
dogma and the appeal to authority, on the historicality of
text and interpretation.

The approaches to the interpretation of dogma sketched
briefly in this chapter are particularly indicative of pre-
World War II Catholic theology. Although such principles of
interpretation reoccur occasionally in contemporary Catholic

tique of the sensus plenior. cf. Loretz, "Die hermeneutische
Grundsätze," 475 who sees in the sensus plenior only a resur-
rection of allegorical interpretation and the critique of
Berkouwer, The Second Vatican Council, 137-138.

[61] Brown, "The Problems of the 'Sensus Plenior,'" "ETL 43
(1967), 460-469. Cf. similar reservations in Brown's article
on biblical interpretation in the Jerome Biblical Commentary,
616.

thought, especially the form-content distinction, they are
more clearly seen today to be continuations of an earlier unhistorical approach to tradition in general and to those specific elements of tradition which are the dogmas of the Church.
A shift away from the classical form of Catholic theology was
produced, above all, by the entry of historical awareness into
Catholic theology in the forties and fifties of this century.[62]
With this transition in theology has come a new appreciation
of the historicality of dogmatic statements.[63]   Dogmatic theology is now in the process of redefining its nature and method
in light of historical awareness. As noted in the first chapter, however, this turn to history has not produced as yet a
significant literature on the hermeneutic of dogma and especially one formulated in light of the Protestant and philosophical hermeneutical discussions. What has been indicated
is the need of a reformulation of the hermeneutic of dogma from
a properly historical and hermeneutical perspective.

---

[62]For an analysis of this shift see, e.g., David Tracy,
The Achievement of Bernard Lonergan (New York: Herder, 1970),
pp. 192ff.

[63]For examples of such an awareness of the historicality
of dogma see H. R. Schlette, "Dogmengeschichte und Geschichtlichkeit des Dogmas," MüThZ 14 (1963), 243-252; Walter Kasper,
"Geschichtlichkeit der Dogmen?" Stimmen der Zeit 179 (1967),
401-416; Josef Finkenzeller, "Überlegungen zur Sprachgestalt
und zur Grenze des Dogmas," MüThZ 21 (1970), 216-236.

CHAPTER III

THE CONTEMPORARY HERMENEUTICAL DISCUSSION

I.   Introduction

The analysis of the problems of tradition and of dogma
in the preceding chapters has pointed directly to the hermeneutical problem. The affirmation of the authority of dogma
and of its character as revealed truth raises without resolving the problem of its interpretation. This is particularly evident in some of the classical approaches to the interpretation of dogma which stop short of an adequate appreciation of the hermeneutical problem. Moreover, as was
suggested in the first chapter, even in recent Catholic theology, the discussion of the hermeneutical problem, as it
applies to Scripture and to doctrinal tradition, is in a very
early stage of development. Our intention now is to further
this discussion by approaching the hermeneutical problem of
dogma through the philosophical and Protestant hermeneutical
discussions of the modern period.

The hermeneutical problem has asserted itself with force
in the last two centuries. Its impact is most apparent in the
German philosophical tradition extending from Friedrich
Schleiermacher and Wilhelm Dilthey in the last century to the
contemporary work of Martin Heidegger and Hans-Georg Gadamer.
In this development, as Gerhard Ebeling has pointed out, her-

meneutic has moved from its role as an auxiliary discipline in the humanities, dealing with rules for interpretation of texts, to become a central philosophical concern.[1] Not merely rules for interpretation but the basic conditions which make understanding possible constitute the present focus of philosophical interest. How does understanding (Verstehen) take place? What is the continuity between subject and object in interpretation which is the basis of understanding? More specifically, in historical interpretation, how does the historian transcend the limits of his own historical and linguistic horizon to appropriate a horizon of another time? What is the subject matter uniting present and past that makes this "fusion" of historical horizons possible? Fundamental questions of this nature have pointed to hermeneutic as a major philosophical problem, both because it is a method of philosophy itself, and because it is a human activity worthy of philosophical investigation.

The philosophical preoccupation with hermeneutic has been paralleled by a similar interest in Protestant theology, particularly in the Bultmannian school. One result of this shared philosophical and theological interest has been a dia-

---

[1]WF, 317. "...the development from Schleiermacher via Dilthey to Heidegger shows that the idea of a theory of understanding is on the move towards laying the foundation of the humanities, indeed it becomes the essence of philosophy, that hermeneutics now takes the place of the classical epistemological theory and indeed that fundamental ontology appears as hermeneutic." Cf. the comment of Emerich Coreth in Grundfragen der Hermeneutik, 7. "So ist das Problem der Hermeneutik zu einem Grundproblem--vielleicht können wir sagen; zu dem Grundproblem--im philosophischen Denken der Gegenwart geworden."

logue between the two fields which has had a noticeable
impact on modern Protestant theology. The importance of
Martin Heidegger's "hermeneutic of existence" for Rudolf
Bultmann's theology, for example, has been widely recognized
and discussed. Increasingly, a pupil of Heidegger and
Bultmann, Hans-Georg Gadamer, is replacing Heidegger as the
focus of the Protestant hermeneutical discussion, and his
work is beginning to have an influence on Catholic theology
as well. [2] In the survey of contemporary hermeneutic that
follows, Gadamer's work will be the primary focus of attention.
The conviction guiding this choice is that Gadamer has presented the most significant and comprehensive treatment of the
hermeneutical problem in contemporary philosophy. Our analysis of modern hermeneutic will also extend to the closest
theological counterpart to Gadamer's thought, the "new hermeneutic" in post-Bultmannian theology. Both of these hermeneutics can contribute to a formulation of a hermeneutic of dogma.
Such a concentration on the German scene is not intended to
imply that no hermeneutical discussion has occurred outside

---

[2] James M. Robinson, "Introduction," The New Hermeneutic,
69. "In the present situation Dilthey and increasingly
Heidegger are being superseded by the Heidelberg philosopher
Hans-Georg Gadamer, a former pupil of Heidegger and Bultmann,
whose magnum opus grounds the humanities in a hermeneutic
oriented not to psychologism or existentialism, but rather to
language and its subject matter." The "magnum opus" to which
Robinson refers is WM. One important example of the impact
of Gadamer on Catholic thought is the volume on hermeneutic
by the transcendental Thomist Emerich Coreth, Grundfragen der
Hermeneutik. Günther Stachel has observed that the post-
Vatican II Catholic hermeneutical discussion is in large part
a product of the encounter with Gadamer's work. Die neue
Hermeneutik, 61.

Germany. In fact, the quite different movements of Anglo-
American and German philosophy demonstrate in recent years a
common concern with the hermeneutical problem.[3] Linguistic
analysis has adopted a "functional" approach to language
which attempts to ground the meaning of words in the historical and experiential contexts in which they are used or "function." To approach the meaning of words in this full historical and existential framework points directly to the hermeneutical problem. The limits of this study prevent a full consideration of the hermeneutical discussion in analytical philosophy. Instead, our focus will be on the work of Gadamer and
the New Hermeneutic following a brief survey of the historical
background to the contemporary hermeneutical discussion.

II. Historical Background: The Emerging Awareness of
    Historicality

    At the beginning of modern hermeneutic stands the work of
Friedrich Schleiermacher.[4] Schleiermacher was the first to

_____

[3]See, e.g., the analysis of this growing mutuality of hermeneutical interest in Coreth, Grundfragen der Hermeneutik, 41ff.
"Durch diese Ausweitung des Sprachproblems nähert sich gegenwär-
tig die analytische Philosophie in mancher Hinsicht nicht nur
der Phänomenologie des späten Husserl mit seinem Problem der
'Lebenswelt' sondern trotz der tiefen Verschiedenheit des Ansat-
zes auch einer existenzialen Hermeneutik, in welcher Heidegger
die Sprache im Ganzen des verstehenden In'der'Welt'Seins' zu
begreifen sucht. Denn es geht auch hier darum, die einzelne
sprachliche Äusserung aus ihrer Funktion im Ganzen des mensch-
lichen Lebens als dem konkreten Bedeutungszusammenhang, in dem
sie steht und aus dem sie gesprochen ist, zu verstehen, d.h. aus
dem Ganzen einer 'Welt' als dem Verständnishorizont, der aber
gerade in dem Ganzen der lebendigen Sprache erschlossen ist."

[4]Schleiermacher's primary hermeneutical reflections are in
Hermeneutik, ed. by H. Kimmerle (Heidelberg: C. Winter, 1959).

expand consideration of hermeneutics from its classical role
of locating rules for the interpretation of texts to a consideration of "understanding" in a broad sense. Schleiermacher
sought to illumine the act of understanding written and spoken
language, particularly that understanding embodied in historical and literary interpretation. Individual expressions
could be understood, Schleiermacher believed, only by setting
them in the total life-context (Lebenszusammenhang) from which
they emerged. The whole life and work of an individual, the
influences of his nation, culture and society--all these and
other factors formed the necessary background for interpretation of an individual expression. A reflective analysis of
particular expressions in the light of this total historical
and grammatical context as well as an intuitive or "divinatory"
apprehension of meaning formed the two main elements of understanding as Schleiermacher conceived it. Hermeneutics could
be defined as the "historical and divinatory, objective and
subjective reconstruction of a given expression."[5] In his
later writings, Schleiermacher concentrated on "psychological"
interpretation--the reduplication or reconstruction of the
conscious and unconscious psychological components which lay

For analyses of Schleiermacher and other figures in nineteenth
century hermeneutic see especially Gadamer, WM and the collection of articles on Schleiermacher Schleiermacher as Contemporary (Journal for Theology and Church, vol. 8, New York:
Herder, 1970).

[5]Hermeneutic is "das geschichtliche und divinatorische,
objective und subjektive Nachkonstruieren der gegebenen Rede."
H ermeneutik, I/7, 31ff. quoted in Coreth, Grundfragen der
Hermeneutik, 27.

behind the life-expression of another individual.[6] Understanding was basically a self-transposition into the mind of an author and an empathetic reproduction of his life experience. The psychological similarity of one individual to another, regardless of historical and cultural differences, made this reconstruction possible.

Wilhelm Dilthey, K. J. Droysen, and other nineteenth century thinkers picked up and expanded Schleiermacher's hermeneutical reflections.[7] Dilthey's developments of Schleiermacher's insights, in particular, has had a clear impact on contemporary hermeneutics. One theme dominated Dilthey's writings--the construction of a "critique of historical reason" parallel to the critiques of pure and practical reason by Immanuel Kant. This continuing interest in historical methodology, as well as in method in the human sciences (Geisteswissenschaften) in general, drew Dilthey into an attack on positivism. As Dilthey saw it, positivism overlooked the essential difference between the human and natural sciences. Understanding in the humanities was for Dilthey grounded in a continuity of experience between subject and object. Knowledge of man, because of this experiential continuity, is properly one of understanding (Verstehen)

---

[6] H. Kimmerle believes that the focus on language in Schleiermacher's early writings is closer to the modern hermeneutical discussion than is the "psychological" focus of his later thought. Cf. "Hermeneutical Theory or Ontological Hermeneutic" in History and Hermeneutic (Journal for Theology and Church, vol. 4), ed. by Robert W. Funk (New York: Harper & Row, 1967), especially 109ff.

[7] For a concise presentation of Dilthey's theory of history, see his Pattern and Meaning in History (New York: Harper & Row, 1961).

or reliving human experiences rather than the neutral and objective "explanation" (Erklärung) of cause and effect relationships in a subject matter foreign to the interpreter.[8] The distinction between the natural and human sciences is apparent. Only in the humanities does understanding depend on the psychological continuity of subject and object. More than had Schleiermacher, Dilthey and Droysen sought to emphasize the "objectifications" of mind in historical and social reality. Not just individual minds, but those historical structures created by mind (the "objective mind" in Dilthey's and Hegel's terms) was the object of interpretation. As Gadamer has pointed out, however, the starting point for moving from individual to history was for Droysen and Dilthey, as well as for Schleiermacher, a metaphysic of individuality.[9] They postulated an essential unity between the "I" and the geistliche Welt; the individual is the causitive force in history. Thus Dilthey chose autobiography and biography as the prime sources for investigation.[10] Through the expressions of key individuals of any historical epoch, the Geist or spiritual quality of that period could be interpreted.[11] That hermeneutic which united all of the figures of the nineteenth century

---

[8]"Understanding" was for Dilthey the "rediscovery of the I in the Thou," Pattern and Meaning in History, 67.

[9]WM, 186-187.

[10]Pattern and Meaning in History, 85ff. Cf. Gadamer's discussion of the significance of this focus on individuals rather than on social structures, WM, 210.

[11]Ibid., 85ff.

hermeneutical discussion was one or another variety of psychological interpretation. A metaphysic of individuality
grounded in the structural similarity of all human minds and
experience was accepted as the underlying continuum which
supported the bridge between subject and object--between the
interpreter's "I" and that of the historical figure under
consideration. [12]

Gadamer has noted that the interpretative penetration of
the mind of another individual was for all of the figures in
the nineteenth century hermeneutical discussion an essentially
"aesthetic" undertaking. The interpreter's task was not
qualitative judgment or critique of historical individuals or
periods; rather it was the "reliving" (nachleben) or reproduction (nachbilden) of experience of the past on its own terms.
The historian's "I" did not stand over history as judge; suc-
cessful historical thinking was the loss of self--a submergence
in the past or an Einfühlen. [13] Even where a more rational and
objective critique was undertaken, it did not entail a judgment
of the past, but a structuring of patterns and meanings in
history on the basis of individual experience. Historical
"types" or general qualities of various periods were sought,
but such structuring was completely free of assessment of

---

[12]The influence of the Romantic movement with its emphasis
on the Geist of an age is apparent, just as it is in the German
Catholic thought represented at Tübingen which emphasized the
experiential unity or spirit of Catholic tradition. Such an
emphasis, as Gadamer points out, involves a neglect of the
historicality of human experience.

[13]WM, 198.

worth.[14] One example from Dilthey's writings may make more clear this aesthetical hermeneutic. Luther's religious experience was for Dilthey the historical avenue through which the historian could increase his possibilities of religious experience.[15] The question whether the historian must feel Luther's experience as a <u>claim</u> or <u>demand</u> for a <u>change</u> in his present mode of existence, however, did not arise for Dilthey. The "freedom" opened by history was the quantitative increase in possibilities of lived experience, not the revelation of <u>alternative</u> modes of existence which must be judged true or false and thus claim or have no claim on the present. Similarly, Dilthey's objective construction of historical types was a "neutral" undertaking--a leveling out of the strange and ambiguous in history.[16] Tradition and history remain "out there"--phenomena of the past--to be experienced and understood, but not to stand over the present.

---

[14] <u>WM</u>, 478-479. Gadamer perhaps overstresses the aesthetic side of Dilthey's temperment. The poetic <u>Weltanschauung</u> was supplemented in Dilthey by a philosophical <u>Weltanschauung</u> which was directed toward a knowledge of life's structures in order to correct problems. That this was basically an objective, non-existential concern, is, however, correct. See, e.g., Wilhelm Dilthey, <u>The Essence of Philosophy</u> (Chapel Hill: U. of North Carolina, 1961).

[15] Wilhelm Dilthey, "The Understanding of Other People and their Life Expressions," in <u>Theories of History</u>, ed. by Patrick Gardiner (Glencoe: Free Press, 1959), 221. "The possibility of having religious experiences is circumscribed for me, as it is for most people today. But when I go through the letters and writings of Luther, the opinions of his contemporaries, the acts of religious conferences and councils, and his own official acts, I live through a religious process of such eruptive power, with life and death literally at stake, that it is quite beyond the experience of anyone today. But I can relive it."

[16] <u>WM</u>, 220.

Gadamer has pointed out most forcefully that the aesthetic appropriation of history in nineteenth century hermeneutic is clearly in the Enlightenment pattern of thinking.[17] The Enlightenment ideal was to understand the past "correctly," i.e., rationally, free from all presuppositions, on its own terms. Traditional or "dogmatic" interpretation, especially the Christian interpretation of Scripture, was for Enlightenment thought a distortion of pure reason. The primary obstacle to historical truth and to truth in general was not a particular tradition or group of traditions. Rather, tradition as such was rejected as a dogmatic bias which prevented the free mind from reaching truth. In antithesis to Greek belief that the way to truth is essentially the recovery of forgotten truths, Enlightenment thinkers conceived the task of knowing as the movement into the future, into the unknown, in discovery of the "new" and "better." Knowledge is thus a forward moving, ever improving force in the advance of human culture. This model of thinking and the devaluation of tradition it entails has determined the methodology of the natural sciences in the last two centuries, and, for many thinkers at least, the methodology of the human sciences as well. It is the Enlightenment suspicion of tradition which in part accounts for the rejection of dogma in the modern period. This same Enlightenment attitude determined the positivistic approaches

---

[17]For Gadamer's analysis of the Enlightenment concept of tradition see "Tradition: I. Phänomenologisch," in RGG, 3rd ed. vol. VI, 966-967. Cf. WM, 256-260.

to history in the eighteenth and nineteenth centuries. What is surprising is that Romantic hermeneutic, despite its critique of positivism, finally accepted the Enlightenment outlook. Both the aesthetic "submergence" in history and the Wertfrei construction of types and patterns are essential devaluations of tradition very much in the Enlightenment pattern of thinking. In both approaches, history remains "out there," in the past. What tradition's claim on the present might be, what its claim is on the historian as individual, is left unasked. The possibility that tradition can appear as a "correction" of the present, altering the interpreter's self-understanding in a decisive way, is not seen.

This consideration of the psychological and aesthetical character of nineteenth century hermeneutic has brought us to that point where the distinctiveness of twentieth century hermeneutic can be determined. Modern hermeneutic involves a critique as well as a continuation of the thought of the last century. This is particularly clear in the work of Gadamer. Gadamer's own formulation of a philosophical hermeneutic emerges in the form of an interpretation and critique of the presuppositions of the romantic and historicist hermeneutic of the last century. Romantic hermeneutic was right in turning to human experience to construct a methodology, but its essential weakness, in Gadamer's estimation, is an inadequate analysis of that experience. The underlying presuppositions of a metaphysical unity of individuality and of the "I" as the sole creative force in molding history are not justified. Moreover, they are

counter to a proper understanding of subjectivity. What links
the individual and the "objective mind"? Gadamer contends the
relationship is experienced not so much as an active creation
of the "I," but as a given--a "thrownness." The individual
experiences not just pattern and meaning, but lack of meaning
and contradiction.[18] Past experience and other individuals'
minds cannot be simply relived or reconstructed; there is an
essential "otherness" and strangeness about them which is
evaded only by illegitimate generalization. Thus the historian
cannot simply move through an individual's mind to the world
around him--rather he is given from the beginning a historical
composite of individual and world, a context of meaning rather
than another "I." His task is not mere sympathy (Einfühlen)
or comparison (Vergleichung) but logical assessment of content.[19] The methodological problem is transposed from psychological interpretation to hermeneutic.[20] The mode of trans-
position is via a proper analysis of human experience, particularly of time-experience, and for this analysis Gadamer turns
to phenomenology.

With Husserl's phenomenological analysis of experience,
the phenomenon of man's time consciousness was moved to the
center of philosophical interest. Husserl directed his inves-

---

[18] WM, 222.

[19] WM, 210. Cf. Gadamer, "Verstehen," RGG, 3rd ed., vol.
VI, 1382.

[20] WM, 211. "Es ist das Problem des Übergangs von der
psychologischen zur hermeneutischen Grundlegung der Geisteswissenschaften das hier den entscheidenden Punkt darstellt."

tigations not to an objectively perceived static "I" but to
man's way of thinking in time--to his intentionality. Man's
language was not for Husserl of "timeless" content but was
bound to the situation of the speaker.[21] Gadamer believes,
however, that Husserl, like Dilthey, remained fundamentally on
the speculative level: Dilthey by his speculative view of the
"inner world" of individuality and Husserl by his understanding of the constitution of the historical world in terms of
conscious life (Bewusstseinleben). Husserl's "transcendental
I" remained too much in the tradition of Descartes' abstract
res cogitans; for Gadamer, at least, the methodological problem of reaching this "I" experience remains unsolved by
Husserl. "The immanent data of reflexive interrogated consciousness does not contain the "thou" in a direct and original
manner."[22] Husserl's method, like that of Romantic hermeneutic,
remains a form of Einfühlen, although in a transcendental manner. Neither supplies the methodological bridge between individual consciousness and the historical world. A contemporary
of Dilthey and Husserl, Count Yorck von Wartenburg, recognized
this essential weakness in both men. It was he, Gadamer maintains, who first saw the need for a bridge between individual
self-consciousness (Selbstbewusstsein) and the lived world
(Lebendigkeit).[23]

---

[21] WM, 236.

[22] Ibid. "Die immanenten Gegebenheiten des reflexiv befrag-
ten Bewusstseins enthalten das Du nicht unmittelbar und originär."

[23] WM, 237-240.

Martin Heidegger seized Yorck's insight into the need for analysis of lived reality and developed such a phenomenology in Being and Time. Heidegger's object of investigation is not Husserl's "transcendental I," but Being-in-the-world--Dasein. The fundamental category in Heidegger's analysis is historicality (Geschichtlichkeit)--a category which is of central importance in Gadamer's thought as well. A full exposition of the meaning of historicality is beyond the scope of this study; a summary exposition, however, must be presented because it is determinative in Gadamer's hermeneutic. Man, in Heidegger's terms, does not so much have a history; rather he is history in a radical sense. There is no direct and apparent unity between "I" and world. Man is rather aware of being "there"-- of a "thrownness" (Geworfenheit). He is a stranger to the world as well as to himself.[24] His self-awareness is not of an immediately available and unchanging "I," but of himself in history, in time, and thus constantly in motion from past through present to future. The "now" is that moment of decision in which the individual in "care" (Sorge) chooses a possibility of action, directing himself into the future. This temporality and historicality of Dasein excludes the possibility of a transcendental viewpoint; there is no vantage point outside time from which the overall meaning of existence in general and my existence in particular can be perceived. History is properly apprehended not in abstract scientific terms, but in

---

[24]WM, 260-261.

concrete lived experience--as fate and as the "power of time."[25] History cannot be explained as the creation and direct reflection of the "I." Rather, the individual is himself molded by history and tradition.

The recognition of the historicality of human existence has implications both for the notion of tradition and for historical understanding. Indeed, Gadamer's hermeneutic and that of Bultmannian theology can be characterized as a working out of the hermeneutical implications of historicality. The finitude and uniqueness of concrete individual experience preclude any naive Einfühlen or, in Husserl's terms, Dahinleben of individual experience. Because futuricity and decision characterize authentic existence, "sinking into" the past or "loss of self" are a flight from the historicality of human existence. Historical understanding is not a linking of experiences into a pattern and meaning "out there." Rather tradition emerges in understanding as possibility. The past is Dasein's mode of becoming present to itself. Understanding is not merely "viewing" or neutral objective awareness; it is repetition. As Heidegger puts it:

> The resoluteness which comes back to itself and hands itself down, then becomes the repetition of a possibility of existence that has come down to us. Repeating is handing down explicitly--that is to say, going back into the possibilities of the Dasein that has-been-there. Repetition does not abandon itself to that which is past, nor does it aim at progress. In the moment of vision authentic existence is indifferent to both of these alternatives.[26]

---

[25]Gadamer, Kleine Schriften, I. Philosophie-Hermeneutik (Tübingen: J. C. B. Mohr, 1967), p. 3.

[26]Heidegger, Being and Time (New York: Harper & Row, 1962),

Heidegger transformed the concept of understanding the past from a purely methodological problem to the constitutive way of the self-realization of Dasein.

Gadamer characterizes this existential relationship to tradition as a "belongingness" (Zugehörigkeit), and he contrasts it with the leveling-out of historical particularity by means of analogies of experience (Gleichartigkeit).[27] The Enlightenment flight from tradition reflected in the non-existential relationship to tradition of Romantic hermeneutic overlooks the fact of historicality and thus the intrinsic bond of understanding, self-understanding, and tradition which characterizes the human sciences. "To hear tradition and to stand in tradition, that is evidently the way of truth which is properly found in the human sciences."[28] In other words, Romantic hermeneutic overlooked the situation of man and of all understanding. All interpretation stands in a situation, with a finite perspective or horizon, with the demands of existence at that point in time--all of which become a part of the act of understanding.[29] The hermeneutical task is to clarify the implications of historicality both for the interpreter as well as for the text.

---

pp. 437-438. Understanding is an existential, a constitutive element of Dasein. The phenomenology of existence itself is "hermeneutic." Cf. Coreth, Grundfragen der Hermeneutik, 30-31 and Gadamer, Kleine Schriften, I, 73 for further discussion of the hermeneutical function of tradition.

[27] WM, 247.

[28] Kleine Schriften, I, 42. "Auf Überlieferung hören und in Überlieferung stehen, das ist offenbar der Weg der Wahrheit den es in den Geisteswissenschaften zu finden gilt."

[29] Ibid., 8.

A recognition of the importance of historicality marks the turning point from nineteenth to twentieth century philosophical hermeneutic. A similar point of transition can be seen in the movement of Protestant theology; the decisive change in theological hermeneutic also came with an emphasis on the historicality of human existence. The "hermeneutical manifesto" marking the beginning of this change was Karl Barth's introduction to his commentary on Romans. Barth's work was a clear break with the ideal of "presuppositionless" interpretation embraced by Liberal theology. As James Robinson has pointed out, Barth's commentary raised the concern which has since dominated Protestant hermeneutic--the importance of the subject in interpretation.[30] How is the interpreter related to the subject matter of the scriptural text? How is he claimed by it? In this framework of interpretation, one which recognizes a need to encounter Scripture as revelation or Word of God, a simple "leap" into the past in a positivistic or romantic way cannot be identified with the hermeneutical task. Scripture properly becomes Word of God when it has an existential impact or effect upon the interpreter and upon the Christian community in the present.

Bultmann and his disciples began with Barth's assertion of the importance of the subject in interpretation but have been concerned to explore thoroughly the full hermeneutical implications of this assertion with the aid of philosophy.

---

[30]Robinson, "Introduction," The New Hermeneutic, 22-24.

Ernst Fuchs has observed that the content or subject matter of
revelation in its scriptural form of expression is so stressed
by Barth that he leaves Scripture finally unrelated to the
self-understanding of modern man. The bible becomes more a
report "about" some external facts of revelation than a witness
that claims the interpreter, "revealing" him as he is.[31] Both
a deemphasis of the tensions raised by critical-historical
method, and thus of the "pastness" of Scripture, particularly
in its mythological forms, as well as a neglect of the hermeneutical role of human self-understanding finally call in question
the adequacy of Barth's hermeneutical presuppositions. In the
last analysis, Barth failed to come to terms with the historicality of interpretation--neglecting both the full historical
situation of the text as well as that of interpretation.

Dissatisfied with a simple rejection of Liberal theology,
Bultmann has attempted to appropriate the legitimate liberal
concerns, particularly the full acceptance of critical-historical method. But in addition to the critical determination of
the past meaning of Scripture, Bultmann and his successors have
taken as their primary hermeneutical task the "translation" of
Scripture's meaning into the situation of the interpreter.

---

[31]Ernst Fuchs, Hermeneutik (Stuttgart: R. Müllerschön,
1968), p. 31. A concern with human self-understanding is not
for Fuchs, however, equivalent to a transformation of the content of the Scriptures into anthropology. For a similar critique of Barth by one of Ebeling's former students see Rolf
Schäfer, "Die hermeneutische Frage in der gegenwärtigen Theologie," in Die hermeneutische Frage in der Theologie, ed. by
Oswald Loretz and Walter Strolz, 434-435. With Ebeling,
Schäfer locates the "word-event" in the movement between the
text and the situation of interpretation.

"Demythologization" is one important element in this effort to move between Scripture in its original and occasionally mythological form and the self-understanding of modern man. With Bultmann, Christian hermeneutic shifted from a simple desire to penetrate the meaning of the text to ask instead what the text brings to the interpreter--how it changes him.[32] Beyond this claim on the interpreter as individual, Bultmann further asks how the "claim" of Scripture can be reasserted in proclamation. The movement from text to proclamation is the full movement of interpretation.[33] The need to take account of the preunderstanding brought by a contemporary interpreter to the text has prompted Bultmann and his followers to rely heavily upon philosophical anthropology, particularly that of Martin Heidegger. What is authentic human self-understanding? This question lies behind Bultmann's reliance on Heidegger's phenomenology of human existence as that philosophical account which best clarifies the understanding of existence given with existence itself and that which most resembles the self-understanding at the center of New Testament faith.

---

[32]Fuchs makes this observation. Marburger Hermeneutik (Tübingen: J. C. B. Mohr, 1968), p. 31. Cf. p. 41.

[33]This is especially clear in the New Hermeneutic as James Robinson points out: "The scope of the New Hermeneutic embraces the whole theological enterprise as a movement of language, from the Word of God attested in Scripture to the preached sermon in which God speaks anew, and is not confined to a subdivision within Biblical studies treating of the theory of exegesis." "Introduction," in The New Hermeneutic, 3-4.

124

Although they express a similar desire to take account
of the self-understanding of modern man, Bultmann's successors have been less dependent on Heidegger's existentials.
They have turned from the self-understanding "behind" language
to the phenomenon of language itself as the fundamental hermeneutical concern.[34] The transmission of faith through
history is the reoccurring "word-event" (Ebeling) or "language-
event" (Fuchs) of the encounter with Christ secured in the
movement between text and proclamation. Not just biblical
exegesis but all of theology finally serves this reoccuring
act of interpretation. Moreover, because this hermeneutical
responsibility cannot rest upon a "special" theological hermeneutic, the post-Bultmannians, like Bultmann himself, have
turned to contemporary philosophy for a clarification of the
hermeneutical problem. Both the theological and philosophical
discussions are united in the quest for a universally valid
and ontologically grounded hermeneutic fully cognizant of the
implications of historicality. The most comprehensive and
important investigation of this question to date, and that
which has had a great impact on the new hermeneutic theologians, is the work of Hans-Georg Gadamer.

_____

[34] James Robinson describes the shift in this way: "Thus
one may say that the new hermeneutic, guided by the basic recognition of the historicness of man and of his understanding,
has elevated language and translation, the more historic
dimensions of interpretation, into positions of principle significance in the understanding of hermeneutic." "Introduction," in The New Hermeneutic, 7. This turn to language is
also typical of the later writings of Heidegger.

III. The Philosophical Hermeneutic of Hans-Georg Gadamer

A. The Situation of the Interpreter

Contemporary philosophical and theological hermeneutic share a concern to explore the full hermeneutical implications of historicality. The preliminary implication of this concern is the recognition that historical understanding is not simply a leap into the past; the situation of the interpreter is an intrinsic component of interpretation. In historical understanding the past can only be understood from and by being mediated into the horizon of interpretation. A circular movement between past and present--both an anticipation of and determination of meaning (the hermeneutical circle) lies at the center of historical understanding. An interpreter confronts a text not as a neutral and disinterested spectator, but with questions and presuppositions, with preconceptions and ways of seeing. The meaning of a past work emerges in response to questions put to it from the present.

A careful analysis of the Vorstruktur of understanding has been carried out by Martin Heidegger.[35] The interpreting subject understands in terms of his own concrete experience of being-in-the-world. Phenomena are perceived "as" something-- as "chairs" or "trees"--i.e., by being located within the existing experience, categories, and preconceptions of the interpreter. All understanding depends upon a prepossession

_____

[35]See, esp., Heidegger, Being and Time, 188ff.

(Vorhabe), a preconception (Vorgriff) or a foresight
(Vorsicht) of meaning. "Any interpretation which is to contribute understanding, must already have understood what is
to be interpreted."[36] This hermeneutical circle has special
importance in history and the human sciences which take human
experience as their field of interpretation. Especially in
the Geisteswissenschaften, the final horizon uniting subject
and object in interpretation is the ontological structure of
existence itself. To attack the forestructure of understanding as a "vicious circle" to be avoided at all costs in the
name of scientific objectivity, is simply to misconceive the
nature of understanding: "But if we see this circle as a
vicious one and look out for ways of avoiding it, even if we
just 'sense' it as an inevitable imperfection, then the act
of understanding has been misunderstood from the ground up."[37]
This is not to say that any anticipation of meaning is satisfactory or that the forestructure of understanding is arbitrarily chosen or a product of fancy or imagination. Appropriate anticipations of meaning are worked out in encounter
with the phenomena to be understood so that they reveal rather
than conceal the subject matter.[38] Some preconception or anticipation of meaning, however, is necessary to make understanding itself a possibility.

---

[36]Heidegger, Being and Time, 194.

[37]Ibid.

[38]Ibid., 195.

Rudolf Bultmann took over the Heideggerian analysis of the forestructure of understanding in his own construction of a theological hermeneutic.[39] The preunderstanding (<u>Vorverständnis</u>) of the interpreter is a necessary component in the interpretation of Scripture. Interpretation is grounded in the interest of the interpreter--in the question brought to the text.[40] Put in somewhat different terms, the "preunderstanding" of the interpreter reflects his "living relationship" to the subject-matter directly or indirectly expressed in the text. As the translation of foreign languages indicates, the words of another language become meaningful only as they are seen to refer to common objects of experience. Thus the final common "horizon" or understanding uniting interpreter and the authors of Scripture is the structure of existence itself. A basis of interpretation is the fact that the expositor and author live as men in the same world, with similar structures of experience in relationship to their environment and to their fellow men. In some instances of interpretation, the living relationship to the subject matter may reflect a narrow and

---

[39]See, especially, Rudolf Bultmann, "Is Exegesis without Presuppositions Possible?" in <u>Existence and Faith</u>, ed. by Schubert Ogden (Cleveland: World Publishing, 1960), pp. 289-296, and "The Problem of Hermeneutics," in <u>Essays Philosophical and Theological</u> (London: SCM, 1955), 234-269.

[40]Bultmann, "The Problem of Hermeneutics," 239. "A comprehension--an interpretation--is, it follows, constantly oriented to a particular formulation of a question, a particular 'objective.' But included in this, therefore, is the fact that it is never without its own presuppositions; or, to put it more precisely, that it is <u>governed</u> <u>always</u> <u>by</u> <u>a</u> <u>prior</u> <u>understanding</u> <u>of</u> <u>the</u> <u>subject</u>, in accordance with which it investigates the text."

128

limited area of concern--e.g., in the interpretation of math-
ematical studies of the past. As the attention of the interpreter shifts to texts such as Scripture, which touch upon
fundamental human concerns and interests, however, the living
relationship called for is much broader and more fundamental.
In those texts which express an understanding of existence,
the preunderstanding of existence itself, either naive and
unthematic or reflectively and carefully worked out, becomes
the precondition for understanding. The question brought to
the text is then properly the question of the meaning of life
itself.[41] Following Heidegger's analysis of the historicality
of existence, Bultmann believes that texts which reveal fundamental possibilities of human existence cannot properly be
appropriated in an aesthetic or uninvolved way. The interpreter must feel the past as a "claim" or summons to examine and
judge his own understanding of existence. The great defect of
nineteenth century hermeneutic, as Bultmann sees it, is that
this existentiell relationship to history, even in the work of

---

[41]Bultmann, "The Problem of Hermeneutics," 253. After
running through a variety of approaches to history--objective,
aesthetical, etc.--Bultmann concludes: "Lastly, the object
of interpretation can be established by interest in history
as the sphere of life in which human existence moves, in which
it attains its possibilities and develops them, and in reflection upon which it attains understanding of itself and of its
own particular possibilities." Existentiell understanding
refers to understanding in which the meaning of the interpreter's own existence is involved, the truth of an understanding
is judged as a possibility for one's own life.

Dilthey, was overlooked.[42]   A loss of self in the aesthetic
submergence in history or in the objective portrayal of past
historical "facts" overlooks the essential subjectivity which
must properly enter interpretation. "Presuppositionless"
exegesis is possible only in the sense that meaning is not
forced on a text or judged before interpretation. It does not
mean, however, that an existential involvement with history
can simply be dismissed as a violation of true understanding.
"The 'most subjective' interpretation is in this case the
'most objective,' that is, only those who are stirred by the
question of their own existence can hear the claim which the
text makes."[43] A preunderstanding fully aware of human historicality is that preunderstanding finally required in the
proper interpretation of Scripture. This entails, for scientific and universally valid interpretation, a reflective and
thematic understanding of existence, which Bultmann finds best
expressed in the early philosophy of Martin Heidegger. Interpretation entails, secondly, an existential openness on the
part of the interpreter to the claim of the text.

    This brief sketch of the importance of the category of
historicality in Heidegger's Being and Time and in Bultmann's
theological hermeneutic has set the stage for presenting
Gadamer's thought, for Gadamer's hermeneutic begins with a

---

[42]For examples of Bultmann's critique of nineteenth century hermeneutic see "The Problem of Hermeneutics," 247ff. and
History and Eschatology (New York: Harper & Row, 1957),
pp. 74ff and 124-125.

[43]"The Problem of Hermeneutics," 256; Cf. "Is Exegesis
Without Presuppositions Possible?" 294.

recognition of historicality in order to unfold its hermeneutical implications. The preliminary implication of this
principle for Gadamer, as for Heidegger and Bultmann, is that
all understanding presupposes the situation of the interpreter.
Understanding is not a leap into the other or the past; the
interpreter can only understand from his own situation in the
present. Heidegger's analysis of the forestructure of understanding is important, Gadamer believes, not so much for the
recognition of the existence of prejudgments in all understanding as for the recognition that these prejudgments have a
positive hermeneutical significance.[44] Contrary to the Enlightenment conviction that all prejudgments are a distortion of
interpretation, proper hermeneutical awareness begins instead
with the recognition that preunderstanding is an essential
element of understanding itself.

But where do the prejudgments of the interpreter come
from? Above all, Gadamer maintains, they come from the tradition in which the interpreter is rooted and to which he belongs.
The mind of the interpreter is not a blank slate waiting to be
filled in but includes a fabric of meanings which have been
given to him by his tradition. This body of traditional presuppositions is part of the horizon of interpretation and is
the medium for the encounter with history. "Presuppositionless" understanding is an impossibility: the historicality of
existence carries with it a situation of understanding which is

---

[44]WM, 250.

not simply the active creation of the "I." Dilthey could not
build a bridge from the individual to the historical world
because his a priori of interior experience was inadequate.
The interpreter is given a language, ways of seeing, and
thought forms by his tradition, and these are often as not
prereflectively or implicitly exercised. The individual is
much more the creation of than the creator of history:

> In truth history does not belong to us, but we
> belong to it. Long before we reflect back upon
> ourselves, we understand ourselves in a manner
> of self-understanding in the family, community
> and state in which we live. The focus of subjec-
> tivity is a distorted reflection. The self-
> reflection of an individual is only a flicker in
> the circular flux of historical life. Therefore
> the prejudgments of an individual much more than
> his judgments are the historical reality of his
> being.[45]

The "rehabilitation" of the notion of authority and tradition
which Gadamer attempts is merely a coming-to-terms with this
reality of historical life.

To recognize the place of prejudgments in understanding
is to reassert the importance of authority and tradition
discredited in the Enlightenment and in nineteenth century
hermeneutic. Man lives in history, in tradition and is molded
by them whether he wishes to be or not. The proper relationship to authority is not closing one's eyes, but accepting it

---

[45]WM, 261. "In Wahrheit gehört die Geschichte nicht uns,
sondern wir gehören ihr. Lange bevor wir in der Rückbesinnung
selber verstehen, verstehen wir uns auf selbstverständliche
Weise in Familie, Gesellschaft und Staat, in denen wir leben.
Der Fokus der Subjektivität ist ein Zerrspiegel. Die Selbst-
besinnung des Individuums ist nur ein Flackern in geschlossenen
Stromkreis der geschichtlichen Lebens. Darum sind die Vorur-
teile des einzelnen weit mehr als seine Urteile die geschichtliche Wirklichkeit seines Seins."

132

consciously and reflectively in a personal acknowledgment.[46]

Tradition and authority are not tyrannical masters, necessarily distortive, rather they are acknowledged guides into truth, always open to criticism and revision. This positive assessment of tradition has led some critics of Gadamer to see in his respect for the role of tradition merely a blind uncritical obedience. Gadamer's response is that a proper relationship to tradition is raising the prejudgments imposed by it to the level of conscious awareness and thus properly opening them to criticism or acceptance. Neglect of one's tradition removes from the beginning the possibility of meaningful criticism and thus of "true" understanding.[47]

The Enlightenment suspicion of tradition and of the prejudgments imposed by it is legitimate to the extent that interpretation can and has been characterized by eisegesis, a simple "reading in" of presupposed meanings into historical texts.

---

[46] WM, 261-264.

[47] Kleine Schriften, I, 120-121. An explicit critique of Gadamer at this point has come from Jürgen Habermas. For the key statements in the debate see Habermas, "Zur Logik der Sozialwissenschaften," Philosophische Rundschau, Beiheft 5, Kap. III (Tübingen: J. C. B. Mohr. 1967). Cf. Gadamer's response in "Rhetorik, Hermeneutik und Ideologiekritik: Metakritische Erörterungen zu Wahrheit und Methode," in Kleine Schriften, I, 113-120. Gadamer's article appeared in English translation in Continuum 8 (1970), 77-95 and a "Summation and Response" by Habermas in the same volume of Continuum, 123-133. The following quotations are from the Continuum articles. Habermas argues that Gadamer presupposes the truth of the consensus represented in the tradition. Authority and reason stand in a symbiotic relationship. Gadamer's mistake, Habermas believes, is overlooking the possibility that the consensus of tradition emerged not as a product of free dialogue and rational choice, but under compulsion or force, and thus represents an illusion rather than the truth. An appropriate approach to tradition is critical, in the Enlightenment pattern, presupposing the possibility of error.

To recognize this possible distortion in the use of prejudgments is not, however, to rule out any and all prejudgments,
but to raise the question of how to distinguish proper pre-
judgments--those which open the interpreter to the subject
matter of texts--from those which close the mind to real understanding. An arbitrary choice of presuppositions as well as
a reliance on prejudgments not open to criticism or revision
means finally that the interpreter is not open to the challenge
of the text. The claim or question posed by the texts is
properly apprehended only when the interpreter is open to new
and unexpected meanings which may in fact shatter his preconceptions. Such an openness to the unexpected is not equivalent to the elimination of prejudgments as such. It points

---

   Every consensus, therefore, in which the understanding of meaning terminates, stands fundamentally under
   the suspicion of being pseudo-communicatively induced:
   the ancients called it delusion, when, under the
   appearance of factually having come to an agreement,
   misunderstanding perpetuated themselves untouched. (125)
"Reason," as reflection and rational discourse, is more appro-
priately the "rock" upon which authorities are crushed than the
"rock" upon which they are founded. (127) Hermeneutic properly passes over into a critique of "ideology"--of traditional
presuppositions which are, in fact, illusion. Gadamer argues,
in contrast, that understanding is better grounded on a prejudgment of truth than of error: "reflection is not always
and unavoidably a step toward dissolving prior convictions."(88)
Habermas' emancipation from authority is far from "the traditional purpose and starting point of the hermeneutical problematic with all its bridge building and recovery of the best in
the past." (84ff.) This positive attitude toward tradition
comes closer to the concrete Christian understanding of its own
tradition, we would suggest. Moreover, Gadamer recognizes the
possibility that hermeneutical reflection can lead to a critique of and even a rejection of an element of tradition, even
though this is the exception rather than the rule.

instead to the search for an authentic preunderstanding, reflectively controlled, and open to the subject matter that
comes to expression in the act of interpretation.[48]

B. The Situation of the Text

Just as the interpreter must be aware of his own historicality in interpreting history, and of the prejudgments it
entails, so he must also be aware of the historicality of the
text. Traditional texts necessarily reflect a horizon different from that of the present day. A past expression, spring-
ign as it does from another situation has a strange or foreign
quality, and part of historical awareness is a recognition of
the pastness of texts. At the same time, however, historical
horizons are not self-contained and totally cut off from one
another. A living continuity of meaning, a tradition, joins
present and past. This takes the form, in the broadest sense,
of a shared world-experience. Heidegger and Bultmann, as we
have seen, focus on the shared experiential structures of
being-in-the-world which join individuals of different historical epochs. An ontology of _Dasein_ is for both the avenue to
the reappropriation of the past. Gadamer points more explicitly beyond these general "existentials" of experience to the
particular concrete traditions that also form the continuity
of present and past. The Christian interpreter, for example,
stands in a Christian tradition, sharing a content or subject

---

[48]_WM_, 253-254. An authentic reliance on prejudgments properly occurs within the framework of a methodical and controlled process of understanding.

matter with the texts of Scripture and other texts of the
Christian past. Christian interpretation points to more than
the past in itself--it points as well to this continuing tradition of Christian faith. Hermeneutic is directed to uncovering such realms of shared meaning, both in reference to the
situation of the interpreter and that of the text. It is the
movement between the strange, historical objectivity of the
text and the belongingness to a tradition. "In this inter-
mediate realm is the true place of hermeneutic."[49]

Gadamer's reference to shared "meaning" or "content"
implies the rejection of the Romantic notion of understanding.
Historical texts do not speak immediately and directly as a
"thou"--as an autobiographical life-expression of an individual. Rather they take on, in a sense, a life of their own.
They attain an openness in two directions which extends their
meanings beyond the conscious intention of the author. In
the first place, they bring to expression not only a clear
assertion of an author, but a realm of meaning as well which
is unspoken, implied or presupposed. The situation of a text,
just as the situation of an interpreter, is always more than
that which can be consciously and reflectively experienced
and expressed. In the second place, the transmission of a
text in tradition expands its original meaning as it enters

---

[49]WM, 279. "Die Stellung zwischen Fremdheit und Vertraut-
heit, die die Überlieferung für uns hat, ist das Zwischen
zwischen der historisch gemeinten abständigen Gegenständlichkeit
und der Zugehörigkeit zu einer Tradition. In diesem Zwischen
ist der wahre Ort der Hermeneutik."

136

and is interpreted in different historical situations.
Written language, particularly, is given a certain "ideality"
of meaning, a "lastingness" which, in contrast, for example,
to an emotional outburst, continues as long as the text
exists.[50] It is this ongoing tradition-process which provides
the medium for subsequent historical encounters with the original text.

By emphasizing the historicality both of interpreter and
text, Gadamer hopes to avoid the pitfalls of Romantic hermeneutic. Understanding is neither an immersion in the past--
a loss of self--based on a naive elimination of the foreignness of all historical expression, nor is it a neutral apprehension of a context of meaning "out there." The question
addressed to the text is molded both by the present situation
of the interpreter and by the historical reality of the text.
It is an anticipation of a shared realm of meaning which
might emerge in the language of tradition. It is thus grounded
neither in pure intuition nor solely in the mind of the author,
but in the anticipation of a shared relationship to truth.[51]
The Romantic attempt to rebuild or relive the past on its own
terms is a hopeless enterprise, based on a neglect both of the
historicality of interpreter and of text. To fix the meaning
of a text at a moment in time--by a canon of mens auctoris or

---

[50]WM, 370. Cf. 372-373. "Unser Einsicht in das Wesen der
literarischen Überlieferung enthält darüber hinaus eine grund-
sätzliche Einrede gegen die hermeneutische Legitimation des
Begriffs des ursprünglichen Lesers."

[51]WM, 277.

of the "original reader"--is to neglect the nature of all understanding. Because understanding is a sharing of meaning between
subject and object, between past and present, there is not a
single meaning to a text.[52] Different situations, different
perspectives will open up differing facets of the "matter" or
content which comes to expression. Gadamer does not wish to
label such "new" understandings as "better" and thus fall into
the false Enlightenment assumption of a continuing advance in
knowledge. Rather they are different: "It is enough to say
that one understands differently if one understands at all."[53]

The time-difference between an historical expression and
interpreter is more for Gadamer than a hurdle to be surmounted.
It is the prime component in the foreign or strange quality of
a past tradition which counteracts any naive identification
with or sinking into the past. The time-difference accentuates
the historicality of understanding. "Truly historical thinking must include in its thought its own historicality."[54] The
strangeness of the past assists the interpreter to make clear
what is different about his own horizon and thus to raise his
own prejudgments to the level of conscious reflection. "True"
understanding, open to control and verification, is based on

---

[52]Kleine Schriften, I, 92.

[53]WM, 280. "Es genügt zu sagen, dass man anders versteht,
wenn man überhaupt versteht."

[54]WM, 281. "Ein wirklich historisches Denken muss die
eigene Geschichtlichkeit mitdenken."

138

a certain amount of separation.[55] Such a separation allows the "true" meaning of a text to arise by serving as a "filter" of the subjective interest of the interpreter and as a guarantee of a proper question.[56]

C. Effective History (Wirkungsgeschichte)

Gadamer refers to the proper method of historical understanding as "effective-history" (Wirkungsgeschichte).[57] Concisely stated, Wirkungsgeschichte is the controlled fusion of horizons. Every historical situation and the historicality of every speaker and hearer assign a certain fixity to possibilities of understanding. Prejudices, prejudgments, ways of thinking, the concepts available in a particular language--all impose a certain "horizon" or limit to one's understanding and experience. As was already indicated, the time difference of the interpreter and text accentuates this fact of understanding. Effective-historical consciousness involves the confrontation of one horizon with another, "sketching" the past horizon in all its uniqueness and the uniqueness of the horizon of the present. The question addressed to the text is the product then not solely of the interpreter's creative imagination, a

---

[55]WM, 282.

[56]Ibid. A critique of Gadamer's notion of the "truth" of interpretation by Eric Hirsch will be examined in chapter five.

[57]Wirkungsgeschichte is difficult to render in English, and "effective history" is at best a faltering attempt. In his first discussion of the term (WM, 283ff.) Gadamer contrasts it to the objective method of Historicism which overlooked the historicality of text and interpreter. Wirkungsgeschichte, in contrast, keeps this historicality in mind, allowing the unique-

reading into the past, nor the past question of the text, but
an anticipation of that realm of meaning shared by interpreter
and text, of the tradition which joins them. The fusion
(Verschmelzung) of present and past horizons, allowing the
"true" content to emerge, is the accomplishment of effective-
history. "We designate the controlled accomplishment of such
a fusion as the task of effective-historical consciousness."[58]

Essential to such understanding is the "application"
(Applikation, Anwendung) of the past to the present. The meaning of a text emerges only when it is effective--when it truly
says something now. Juridical and theological hermeneutic provide the key examples cited by Gadamer of such application. A
system of laws or a single law emerge in legal interpretation
not as they were--as an unchanging past reality--but in application to a concrete case now. This concretion of meaning
broadens the former meaning of the text, not as an arbitrary
addition of content, but as a working out of implicit possibilities of meaning in the law itself.[59] Similarly, theological
understanding is properly directed toward proclamation. Scriptural interpretation, for example, is fulfilled in a renewal of
the event of faith present in the text at hand. This is so not

---

ness and strangeness of the text to remain while seeking the
shared tradition and the text's "effect" or claim on the present. The true reality (Wirklichkeit) of history is sought,
therefore, and not a meaning read into the past or the meaning
"back there."

[58]WM, 290. "Wir bezeichneten den kontrollierten Vollzug
solcher Verschmelzung als die Aufgabe des wirkungsgeschicht-
lichen Bewusstseins."

[59]WM, 214-215.

140

merely because of a responsibility of the interpreter to his community, but because the text itself is directed at such communication. Application is no after thought, a supplement to understanding, but an intrinsic component in the act of understanding itself.[60]

The high-form of the effective-historical consciousness is a willingness to listen. Historical understanding is not a tyranny of present over past or past over present, but a conversation in which the true reality of man emerges.[61] The "belongingness" to tradition that Gadamer emphasizes is essentially a willingness to hear what the other says: "Belonging to another means always at the same time ability to hear another."[62] Tradition is thus a partner in communication (Kommunikationspartner) which addresses us not as past event, but as a "thou" in language.[63] To avoid the Romantic delusion of an I as the object of understanding, Gadamer emphasizes the linguistic content of tradition; it is a context of meaning which must be brought to expression (Zum-Reden-Bringen). Tradition is never, therefore, over and done with; never simply Historie. It is ever-anew brought to expression in changing situations of understanding and thus remains infinitely open.

---

[60]WM, 323.

[61]Kleine Schriften, I, 157.

[62]WM, 343. "Zueinandergehören heisst immer zugleich Auf-ein-ander-Hörenkonnen."

[63]WM, 340.

The prevalence of linguistic terms in Gadamer's hermeneutic offers an indication of the foundation of his thinking in
a view of language. As James M. Robinson has recognized, the
decisive step Gadamer takes beyond the Dasein analysis of
Heidegger in Being and Time is in his orientation of the hermeneutic problem to "language and its subject matter."[64] The
basic structure of Being-in-the-world for Gadamer is linguistic.
There is a unity of human world-experience (Welterfahrung) and
the origin of language. Language is essentially prereflective,
so synonomous with thought that it is extremely difficult to
separate the two in our individual experience. The givenness
of language is the underlying structure of the givenness of
tradition. The coming-to-expression of a shared realm of truth
in the effective-historical fusion of horizons is a linguistic
event:

> As the things, the characteristics and unity consti-
> tuting our experience of the world come to expression,
> so is the tradition which comes to us brought once
> again to language in which we understand and inter-
> pret it. The linguisticality of this coming-to-
> expression is the linguisticality of human world-
> experience in general. It is that which has finally
> led our analysis of the hermeneutic phenomenon to
> the discussion of the relationship of language and
> world.[65]

The givenness of man's historical situation is profoundly the
givenness of his language. Each individual stands in a language
just as he stands in history and in a world. With his language
he is given a way of looking at the world, a horizon of under-

---

[64]Cf. footnote #34.

[65]WM, 432.

standing, which is transcended not by introspection but by conversation.[66] The freedom to rise above his environment, including his tradition, distinguishes man from the animals, and is the basis for the multiplicity of languages. At the same time, however, there is a basic unity of languages, because they reflect not just isolated egos, but the juncture of man and world. Thus linguistic communities with a certain unity of language and experience are a part of Being-in-the-world: "All forms of living communities are forms of linguistic communities--even more than this, they build language."[67]

The communal nature of man's existence, his essential Mitmenschlichkeit, and "belongingness" to tradition impart a necessary "I-lessness" to language.[68] Language is not merely individual self-expression; it is fundamentally Zu-Sprache. The continual reawakening of shared agreement in understanding (Verständingung in Verstehen) which characterizes the historicality of man is the product of conversation (Gespräch). As the discussion of Wirkungsgeschichte indicates, the other in understanding is not used as a tool; he is a partner in communication. The Sache emerges in understanding as a product of dialogue, not of domination. The nature of conversation is openness; what emerges in the course of its unfolding cannot be predetermined but transcends what each partner brings. A shared

---

[66]WM, 419.

[67]WM, 422. "Alle Formen menschlicher Lebensgemeinschaft sind Formen von Sprachgemeinschaft, je mehr noch: sie bilden Sprache."

[68]Kleine Schriften, I, 97ff.

realm of meaning is secured in authentic conversation which is
the product of a union of minds and which has a certain life
or existence of its own. Gadamer's use of the phrase zu-
Sprache-kommen implies the passivity, in a way, of the partners
in dialogue. Meaning "emerges" or "comes-to-expression"; it
is not forced by one individual on the text or other person.
Gadamer's analysis of Spiel (play, game) in his ontology of
art points to this basic structure of understanding. A participant in a game loses the meaning if he stands outside as a
spectator. The meaning of a game comes to expression in the
formation of a common world of meaning by the players. Similarly, the beholder of a play understands when he allows the
meaning of the work to come to expression or find its way into
his mind. He is the one "playing" the game (the Spielende).[69]
In an analogous way, the understanding of another person or of
a text is grounded not in neutral observation, in viewing or
taking a look, but in hearing. Hearing, for Gadamer, has a
precedence over seeing as the faculty that most characterizes
the reality of man. There is an uncontrollability, a necessary
openness in hearing that is not present in sight. In seeing,
one can look in a particular direction, limit his perspective;
hearing is a more passive and consequently a more open basis
for understanding.

Openness to understanding characterizes the proper historical frame of mind. Gadamer seeks no closed view of history

---

[69]WM, 104-105.

144

which eliminates the need for new interpretation. History "in itself" is not attainable by man; only an everbroadened perspective of history open to new acts of understanding. The "belongingness" to tradition which characterizes man is the constant willingness to engage in conversation with the past, and in this conversation, in the fusion of horizons it entails, to feel the claim of the subject-matter that emerges. There is no gradual perfecting of knowledge which excludes the need to return to the past; truth emerges not as a completed, self-contained content but as a way of being, as the fulfillment of an understanding which is always in motion.[70]

IV. The New Hermeneutic

The impact of Gadamer's hermeneutic on contemporary theology is just beginning to be felt. At the moment, the closest theological counterpart to Gadamer's thought is the work of those post-Bultmannians in the "New Hermeneutic." Gerhard Ebeling and Ernst Fuchs, the major spokesmen for the movement, have relied upon the philosophies of Gadamer and Heidegger, although they have been less willing than their mentor, Rudolf Bultmann, to acknowledge their philosophical dependencies. As James M. Robinson, the most knowledgeable commentator on the New Hermeneutic, has pointed out, however, the continuity between the New Hermeneutic and Gadamer's thought is apparent, so much so that Gadamer can be said to have replaced Heidegger as the focus of the Protestant hermeneutical discussion.[71]

---

[70]WM, 359.

[71]Cf. footnote #2 in this chapter.

This continuity is evident at a number of points.

In the first place, as the very title of the movement indicates, "hermeneutic" stands at the center of theological interest for the Bultmannians just as it stands at the center of philosophical interest for Gadamer. The responsibility of theology as a whole, not just of biblical exegesis and Church history, is the hermeneutical movement between the texts of Christian tradition and the situation of modern man. The exegetical and theological task is to assist the "word-event" (Ebeling) or "language-event" (Fuchs)--the movement from text through proclamation to faith. The scope of the New Hermeneutic "embraces the whole theological enterprise as a movement of language, from the Word of God attested in scripture to the preached sermon in which God speaks anew, and is not confined to a subdivision within Biblical studies treating of the theory of exegesis."[72] By its very nature, Christian theology is bound to a textual tradition--to Scripture, above all, but also to a textual tradition in the post-biblical history of the Church. The continuing obligation of theology is one of "translation" of the tradition of Christian faith into the changing situation of belief. Thus theology encompasses both a historical dimension, an attentiveness to the textual tradition of faith, and a dogmatic or systematic concern to illumine the existence of contemporary man in the encounter with the Word of God. The basic structure of understanding analyzed by

---

[72]Robinson, "Introduction," The New Hermeneutic, 3-4.

Gadamer is here reasserted in a Christian context; "hermeneutical theology" moves between the horizon of texts and horizon of interpretation.[73]

An awareness of the situation of the texts of faith is intrinsically connected for both Ebeling and Fuchs to the acceptance of critical historical method.[74] One clear conclusion of the Bultmannian hermeneutical discussion is that there is no "special" hermeneutic for Scripture. Both the sola fide principle and modern historical method, as indicated in the first chapter, do not permit the interpreter to attribute any qualitative uniqueness to the language of the Bible. "The exposition of the Bible as the most important of all books is in principle carried out in exactly the same way as the exposition of any other book."[75] Consequently, the hermeneutical problem is shared by theology with all of the Geisteswissenschaften involved in the interpretation of human expressions of experience. At the foundation of this generalization of hermeneutical concern is the work of Schleiermacher and Wilhelm Dilthey:

> ...the development from Schleiermacher via Dilthey
> to Heidegger shows that the idea of a theory of
> understanding is on the move towards laying the
> foundation of the humanities, indeed even becomes
> the essence of philosophy, that hermeneutics now

---

[73]Ebeling, "Hermeneutische Theologie," in Wort und Glaube, Bd. II (Tübingen: J. C. B. Mohr, 1969), p. 87.

[74]See Ebeling's programmatic essay, "The Significance of the Critical-Historical Method for Church and Theology in Protestantism," WF, 17-61.

[75]WF, 427.

> takes the place of the classical epistemological
> theory, and indeed that fundamental ontology
> appears as hermeneutics.[76]

The "immersion" of revelation in history explains for Fuchs this bond of Christian hermeneutics to historical method and universal hermeneutics. The paradox of the Christian claim is the full presence of revelation in human language and experience.[77] The "historicity" of revelation also makes it impossible for Ebeling to define the content of revelation in such a way as to remove Scripture from the field of historical criticism.[78] This bond of Christianity to history can present difficulties to the interpreter when the foreignness or strangeness of authoritative texts becomes apparent--as, for example, in the interpretation of mythological expressions. But such difficulties do not alter the fact that an essential dimension of the hermeneutical process is locating scriptural texts in their past horizon.

The acceptance of critical historical method is not equivalent to the acceptance of the positivistic vision of history. Like Gadamer, the New Hermeneutic theologians question those models of historical understanding which leave the past as past and which conceive the task of understanding as the amassing of "facts" about the distant and irrelevant course of the events of history.[79] Nor is hermeneutic properly conceived in the

---

[76]WF, 317.

[77]Fuchs, Hermeneutik, 95ff.

[78]Ebeling, The Problem of Historicity, 73-74.

[79]Ebeling, Theology and Proclamation (Philadelphia: Fortress, 1966), p. 17.

Romantic effort to achieve contemporaneity with authors of the past.[80] Historical understanding is not simply a "leap" into the past--either by the objective reconstruction of history as it really was or by the subjective reliving of the experience of an author. A correct description of the course of history which leaves aside the question of the truth of the text _for the interpreter_ has missed the point of interpretation.[81] Real interpretation involves both the recognition of the historical particularity of the text and an encounter or confrontation in an existential way. Interpretation properly translates the original "claim" of the text--its power to demand decision and affect self-understanding.

A concern to preserve the claim of the text and the "event" character of the Word of God directs Ebeling and Fuchs, as it did Bultmann, to take account of the _subjectivity of the interpreter_: the differentiating factor in interpretation is the question brought to the text. The hermeneutical importance of preunderstanding, philosophically analyzed by Heidegger and Gadamer, becomes a central concern in the New Hermeneutic as well. But the interpreter's self-understanding is for both Ebeling and Fuchs not only the avenue to interpretation, it is also the _goal_ of the hermeneutical process. For this reason both Ebeling and Fuchs refer to self-understanding

---

[80]Robinson makes this observation in "Introduction," _The New Hermeneutic_, 59.

[81]Fuchs, _Hermeneutik_, 108-109. Cf. _Marburger Hermeneutik_, 37-38. The "truth" of a text is reached when the text emerges in the interpreter's experience as an event. "Wir fragen nach der Wahrheit, indem wir fragen, _wo_ sie _erscheint_. Wir lassen

as the hermeneutical principle for the interpretation of
Scripture. Understanding properly occurs when the interpreter
reads the text as a summons to examine his self-understanding
and to change it in light of the text. Hermeneutic is thus
as much exposition by as it is exposition of the text. The
"question about ourselves" functions for Fuchs as that hermeneutical principle which one sets before the text to allow
it to come to expression.[82] Similarly, Ebeling identifies
the "conscience" as the basis of interpretation: "The hermeneutic principle of proper exegesis of holy scripture is therefore
man as conscience."[83] For Ebeling as for Fuchs, human self-
understanding under the "law" before illumination by the
Gospel is essentially an awareness of need, of sin, of a lack
of identity with oneself.[84] Human existence is characterized
by a questionableness, a lack of meaning, to which the Christian proclamation comes as an answer. Conscience leads ultimately to a deep awareness of the "sting" of the law. This
preunderstanding opens man to the real meaning and truth of
the texts of Scripture. God's word is fulfilled not in the
communication of abstract truths, but in its radical effect
on human self-understanding as it communicates the meaning of

---

uns nicht im voraus logisch gefangennahmen, sondern fragen nach
der Situation der Wahrheit. Das ist das Besonder der "neuen"
Hermeneutik."

[82]Fuchs, Hermeneutik, 118-139.

[83]WF, 428.

[84]WF, 422.

existence. It is addressed not to man's objective reason,
but to man in his true subjectivity, and only by touching
the subject does God's word emerge as event. This event
character of interpretation is not finally the product of
critical historical awareness, for Scripture, as a historical document, must to some extent be set off as an object in
historical analysis. For this reason, it is not the written
word of Scripture which is properly Word of God, but rather
the oral word of proclamation.[85] To the essence of the Word
belongs its oral character, i.e., its character of an event
in personal experience.

Ebeling and Fuchs define the faith preunderstanding of
the interpreter chiefly in terms of his concern for the word-
event of proclamation. The movement from past to present
proclamation is at the heart of the hermeneutical problem and
is made possible by what Ebeling and Fuchs call "existiantia-
list interpretation," --interpretation of the text "with regard to the word-event."[86] The sermon is the execution or
application of the text. By it the text becomes more than a
past fact or expression of another time, it becomes "a hermeneutic aid in the understanding of present experience.[87] Basic
to this focus on proclamation is the Bultmannian conviction
that authentic human existence is finally not a product of an

[85]WF, 429.
[86]WF, 331.
[87]Ibid.

individual decision, of "resolve" or "courage." It instead
springs from a summons (<u>Anrede</u>) which comes to man from outside himself.[88] Proclamation is this summons, the place
where the real being of man is realized and achieved.[89]

Apparent throughout the writings of the New Hermeneutic,
as in the work of Gadamer, is a focus on the <u>importance</u> <u>of</u>
<u>language</u> in the hermeneutical process. Language makes under-
standing possible and thus, even when obscure, has an essentially positive function. Language of the past, even the
mythical language of the Bible, is not primarily a block to
understanding, as Bultmann's notion of demythologizing seems
to imply. While Bultmann's emphasis is on the understanding
of existence behind the language of the Bible, his successors
emphasize the ongoing language or word event in tradition as
the biblical texts come to expression in changed situations
of understanding. The hermeneutical task is simply to help
the text itself to come to expression, which, in the case of
Scripture means allowing the text to fulfill itself in proclamation. Only when the language of the Bible has found new
expression in the language of proclamation is the circle of
understanding complete. The act of understanding is characterized by an unbroken linguisticality in the passage from
language "then" to language "now."

---

[88]Fuchs, <u>Hermeneutik</u>, 73-74.

[89]<u>Ibid.</u>, 56-57. "Die existentiale Interpretation deckt
auf, dass gerade der schuldige Mensch ein <u>angeredeter</u> und
<u>anzuredender</u> Mensch ist, dass also unsere Existenz primär nicht
auf das Sehen, sondern auf das Hören bezogen ist."

Several hermeneutical implications are drawn by Ebeling from his positive assessment of language:[90] 1) Hermeneutical theory is concerned only with those texts where the "word-event" is hindered for some reason or other. This hindrance may be overcome by simply grammatical or philological interpretation, by, at a further extreme, an analysis of the basic conditions which make understanding possible, or by an act of understanding somewhere between these two extreme possibilities; 2) Since hermeneutics exists only to further the word's own intelligibility, it must be fundamentally a theory of language. Pointing to the same reality as that defined by the Greek notion of Logos, hermeneutics must elucidate those universal conditions--the basic continuity of world-experience-- which make understandable words possible; 3) In addressing itself to language, hermeneutic necessarily addresses itself to the reality that comes to expression through language. It is not concerned with mere matters of form or assigning meanings to individual words, but with reaching that content or subject matter that gave rise to word and which transcends it. The very possibility of understanding rests on the interpreter's participation in and previous understanding of the subject matter of the text: "Words produce understanding only by appealing to experience and leading to experience. Only where word has already taken place can word take place. Only where there is already previous understanding can understanding take

---

[90]WF, 318-320.

place. Only a man who is already concerned with the matter in question can be claimed for it."[91] Thus the interpretative problem lies as much in the interpreter's relationship to the text as in the language of the text itself. The preoccupation of Ebeling and Fuchs with "conscience," "law," or the "question about ourselves" reflects a concern to locate that preunderstanding which properly opens the interpreter to the subject-matter of the scriptural text. Understanding occurs when, as Gadamer puts it, the right "questions" are addressed to the text. For Ebeling and Fuchs the proper question for the interpretation of Scripture is an awareness of the radical questionability of existence as a whole.

The "word-event" or movement between scriptural text and proclamation has been seized by Ebeling in particular as a schema for uniting the branches of theology in one hermeneutical enterprise. Church history, exegesis, and systematic theology, all in their own way, serve the word-event. Historical theology, as Ebeling sees it, studies the past attempts in Christianity to realize the "word-event." Church history is properly the history of the interpretation of Scripture. This concern with the movement between text and proclamation also characterizes the task of dogmatic or systematic theology, for it must point out not only what was but what is meaningful proclamation: "It is the task of systematic theology, with an open ear to the diversity in the history of language, to work out concepts which take the reality that confronts us--this

---

[91]WF, 320.

aspect now comes to the fore--and give expression to it in
the way it has to be given expression by the Christian message."[92] Exegesis and historical theology are concerned with
explicatio--the exposition of the texts of Christian tradition; systematic theology is concerned with applicatio--locat-
ing the point of contact between the experience of modern man
and the content of Christian faith. Necessarily, the interest
in applying the tradition draws systematic theology close to
the function of proclamation. Like proclamation, systematic
theology is concerned not so much with traditio as with the
actus tradendi. The event of the Word of God now is for both
the primary object of interest and not the investigation of
the past. While proclamation focuses on the concrete word-
event in particular situations, however, dogmatic theology
reflects upon the general or universal conditions which make
the meaningful proclamation possible, as well as upon the con-
ceptualization of Christian belief in systematic form. Finally,
for the New Hermeneutic, this movement to the universal and
theoretical, just as the focus on the past in critical historical interpretation, prevents theology from actually mediating
the word-event. The situation of preaching, not of theology,
is that point at which the Word of God is properly heard.[93]

---

[92]WF, 252; Cf. "Hermeneutische Theologie," 120.

[93]Fuchs, Hermeneutik, 99. "Theologie ist aber nicht
Predigt, sondern setzt die Predigt als Mitteilung von Offenbarung voraus; sie fragt nach der Möglichkeit solcher Mitteilung als einer Tat des Menschen, also darf die Theologie
die Fülle der Offenbarung gar nicht aussagen wollen."

With the event of proclamation, the "effective-historical" path of faith understanding, as the post-Bultmannians conceive it, is complete. The linguistic circle has been completed which fuses the horizon of the biblical texts to that of interpretation. Gadamer, as we have seen, identifies hermeneutic as the central existential in human experience. The avenue to truth is built upon the continuing reappropriation of the past and the application of its truth to the present, as man moves into the future. In the more specific arena of Christian belief, this same centrality of hermeneutic has been asserted by Ebeling and Fuchs. Christian faith persists through time by its continuing hermeneutical reappropriation of its tradition. The movement of faith is from text through understanding to the renewed event of proclamation. In this movement the hermeneutical circle of faith is closed.

V. Summary and Critical Reflections

This chapter has been primarily an exposition of the hermeneutics of Gadamer and of the post-Bultmannians. What follows in this concluding section is both a summary of and critical reflection upon the main themes of the contemporary German hermeneutical discussion as well as an attempt to anticipate some of the ways in which the discussion may be applied in a formulation of a hermeneutic of dogma.

An initial observation is that the rehabilition of tradition carried out by Gadamer suggests as well a reemphasis on the hermeneutical importance of dogma. The importance assigned

by Catholicism, in particular, to its dogmatic prejudgments
is not, as Enlightenment thought assumed, a violation of hermeneutical integrity. A respect for the hermeneutical significance of tradition simply reflects the necessary structure
of understanding. "Presuppositionless" interpretation, as
Blondel also emphasized, simply means interpretation in which
presuppositions unconsciously rather than consciously affect
interpretation. By the nature of historical being, man is
granted a language and is shaped by his environment and education in the mold of a long historical tradition. This is
particularly the case with those prejudgments that have
attained a widely recognized or "classical" importance in a
given tradition. All understanding depends upon the interpreter's prejudgments and questions, supplied in large part
by his tradition, through which he has contact with and inter-
prets the past. To approach doctrinal tradition as a guide to
the truth of Christian faith and as a legitimate "effective-
historical" amplification of the apostolic witness is therefore a valid hermeneutical stance. The presupposition should
be of the truth and importance of doctrinal tradition rather
than of its falsity and irrelevance.

Such a reliance on tradition and authority is not equivalent to legalism or to an inflexible dogmatism. The openness
of the interpreter is an essential element of authentic interpretation. Understanding is distorted when the prejudgments
granted by tradition harden to the point that they are not
open to being broadened or corrected in new acts of understand-

ing. Openness to the subject matter that comes to expression
in interpretation can point to the need to alter a presupposition or traditional view that suddenly appears as distorted
or too one-sided. In such instances, the openness of the interpreter carries the possibility of a correction or dissolution of traditional prejudgments.

The openness of the interpreter is paralleled in hermeneutic by the openness of the text. Such an openness is reflected, first of all, in the fact that understanding has to
do not only with texts but also with the subject matter that
comes to expression in texts. Understanding occurs when interpreter and text share or participate in a common subject
matter or content that transcends what text or interpreter by
themselves bring to the event of interpretation. Such a
transcendence of meaning occurs especially at two levels:
1) What is said or carried along with (mitgesagt) the language
of a text may point to a reality which the author could express
only in a limited or partial way as well as meaning which was
only implicit, not in the author's conscious intention.
2) The effective-historical movement of texts expands their
meaning as they are applied and interpreted in new situations.
Both instances suggest that Sachkritik, criticism in light of
the subject matter, is an appropriate part of interpretation.

The openness of interpreter and of text suggests why
Gadamer identifies dialogue rather than monologue as the appropriate model of historical understanding. Gadamer's emphasis
on the positive significance of the time-difference between

text and interpreter makes it possible for the interpreter to
make clear what is different about his own horizon as well as
the distinctiveness of the horizon of the text. The separation in time allows the proper questions to emerge as well as
exposing those prejudgments which may stand in need of revision.
One advantage of Gadamer's thought at this point is its potential to serve as a corrective to the "psychologism" of Bultmannian hermeneutic. In nineteenth century hermeneutic, the
bridge between the historical interpreter and figures of the
past was grounded in a process of psychological interpretation.
The similarity of human minds made possible a leap from the
present into the past. The temporal gulf between past and
present was broken down to be replaced by a psychological uni-
fication. Both the "otherness" and strangeness of the text and
its claim on the present seemed to disappear. Rudolf Bultmann
contrasts his hermeneutic with that of the nineteenth century
by pointing to his recognition of the "claim" of the text--
the demand placed upon the interpreter for decision. The path
of interpretation he follows to the claim of the text, however,
is quite similar to the "psychologism" of Romantic hermeneutic.
For Bultmann the temporal separation of text and interpreter is
removed by an appeal to the common experiential structures of
being-in-the-world. Heidegger's existentials provide a preunderstanding for the interpretation of any text which expresses
an understanding of human existence. This existential preunderstanding enables Bultmann to circumvent the historical peculi-
arity of the scriptural texts by locating the "authentic" pre-

understanding of existence embodied in them. Bultmann's
encounter with possibilities of existence from the past, even
though on an existential rather than an aesthetical plane, is
not too far removed from the Romantic dissolution of the gap
between past and present.

Gadamer's positive interpretation of the temporal separation of text and interpreter can serve at this juncture to
preserve a recognition of the uniqueness and otherness of
horizons of the past. He approaches the text with no _fixed_
preunderstanding or _inflexible_ hermeneutical principle. The
hermeneutical task as he conceives it is not to locate an
already assumed understanding of existence in the text, but
rather to allow the chance for a previously unrecognized content or subject matter to emerge in the event of interpretation.
There is some of this openness in the "word-event" of post-
Bultmannian hermeneutic. For Gadamer and the New Hermeneutic
theologians, content "comes to expression" in a contingent act
of understanding which cannot be manipulated or automatically
produced. Gadamer succeeds where Ebeling and Fuchs do not,
however, in escaping the tyranny of a fixed hermeneutical principle, whether this is expressed in terms of Ebeling's dialectic of Law-Gospel or Fuch's "question about ourselves." One can
ask whether Ebeling, for example, is finally open to a radical
correction of his Lutheran Law-Gospel understanding. It seems
to function instead as the basic preunderstanding for interpreting all elements of the New Testament canon and for criticizing
those elements of Scripture, such as the Epistle of James,

which do not fit neatly into the Law-Gospel schema. It is not the interpreter's criticism of the New Testament in light of a preunderstanding which is here at fault, but the extent to which this prejudgment is carried to every instance of interpretation and is fundamentally removed from any real criticism or reassessment.

The recognition of the openness of the interpreter and text carries with it a warning against any attempt to locate a definitive meaning for any given text. The structure of hermeneutics suggests instead that a number of levels of meaning and tradition must be differentiated--any of which can become a problem for interpretation. Three such levels of meaning stand out quite clearly in foregoing analysis.

In the first place, one can seek the original historical sense of any given text. What was its meaning in its given historical situation? Critical-historical and philological analysis usually take this level as the primary field of investigation. All questions about the mind of the author, his intentions, the thought forms he employed are directed to uncovering the original meaning of the text. As Gadamer has made clear, however, even this historical focus takes the interpreter beyond the conscious intention of the original author. Language expresses more than conscious intentions. Even at the original level of meaning, the object of investigation is more properly an assessment of content than it is the penetration of the mind of an author to uncover his inner thoughts and intentions.

A second level of meaning is the <u>effective-historical</u> <u>context</u> which makes up the future of any given text. Espe-cially texts of "classical" importance are not restricted in their meaning to the historical situation in which they emerge. They have a continuing impact as they are reappropriated in subsequent historical situations. The meaning assumed by the text at this level transcends the original historical sense, but not as an arbitrary and unwarrented addition of content. Rather, the effective-historical movement opens up implicit meanings in the text itself, as the text provides "answers" to new questions and is unfolded in an ever-broader context of meaning. It is from within and through the continuum of tradi-tion extending from text to interpreter that understanding takes place. The Christian process of tradition, for example, did not stop with the apostolic era. The totality of Church history may be examined, to borrow Gerhard Ebeling's descrip-tion, as the "history of the interpretation of Scripture." Different meanings of the biblical witness emerge as the Church moves through history, reinterpreting and applying its faith in changing situations. This traditional process is not neces-sarily distortive, but the historical "working out" of the con-tent of faith and the basis for reinterpretations along the way of history. What is not clear in the New Hermeneutic is the extent to which this medium of tradition is viewed as a <u>positive</u> contribution to the task of interpretation. <u>Sola</u> <u>scriptura</u> as employed by Fuchs and Ebeling becomes the principle for interpreting and correcting the tradition. The possibility

that tradition can open new perspectives on Scripture, however, is deemphasized. Both the Catholic stress on the hermeneutical function of tradition and the Gadamerian insight
that it is only through tradition that one comes to the
textual origins receive inadequate recognition.

A final level of meaning is the mediation and translation of the text into the situation of the interpreter. The
historical horizon of the text and those of subsequent tradition are different from that of modern man. Bultmann's program of "demythologization" springs from this recognition
that the world view of the biblical authors is not the same
as that of modern man--it must be translated or reexpressed
to communicate in the present age. Such changes in world-
view as well as changes in conceptuality and thought forms
all point to the need for reexpression of tradition in light
of the present.

The differentiation of the three levels of tradition is
not meant to suggest that they are cut off from each other
or that they are appropriated in three distinct acts of
understanding. As Gadamer's analysis of the structure of understanding indicates, the horizon of the original meaning of a
text, the effective-historical context, and the present application all flow together in a unified act of understanding.
The effective historical context points back to its textual
origin, and the original texts are read in light of subsequent
tradition. Some form of application, either implicit or explicit, takes place in all acts of understanding. And present

163

understanding is complete only when formed in light of tradition. Thus the three levels of tradition, while they can be
distinguished, cannot be kept in isolation from one another.
Each reflects a particular aspect of effective-historical
consciousness.

What the differentiation of levels of meaning does indicate, is that it is impossible to locate one timeless and definitive meaning for any given text. Historical understanding
will never be complete, for the total act of understanding
entails the continuing mediation of meaning into a changing
horizon of interpretation. New horizons prompt different
questions and thus open up new levels of meaning in any given
textual tradition. Not only is understanding open into the
future, however, in the sense of the emergence of new questions, history itself is not a fixed and timeless collection
of facts. The continuing reappropriation of the past can
point to forgotten or distorted aspects of tradition. As
Heidegger and Gadamer both stress, the path to truth in the
humanities is through the tradition, in the recovery of "forgotten" truths; it is not a movement in which only the totally
new has significance.

An awareness of the multiplicity of meanings of tradition
and the openendedness of understanding has obvious implications
for the interpretation of dogma which will be developed in the
next chapter. If dogma has a binding and authoritative meaning, at which level of tradition is this meaning located? Can
the meaning of a dogmatic text, its pure essence or content,

be any more successfully located than in the interpretation of other historical sources? Does the effective-historical context of interpretation finally entail a total relativism? A recognition of the full historicality of interpretation points to these and other questions which need more careful examination.

CHAPTER IV

CONTEMPORARY HERMENEUTIC

AND THE INTERPRETATION OF DOGMA

The purpose of this chapter is to suggest some of the
possible contributions of the contemporary German hermeneutical discussion to the formulation of a hermeneutic of
Catholic dogma. The contribution to be expected, as the
preceding chapter indicates, is not a set of rules for the
interpretation of dogmatic texts. Neither Gadamer nor the
New Hermeneutic has provided a precise method in the form of
hermeneutical axioms or rules for interpretation. What they
have presented instead is a clarification of the basic structure of historical understanding. Gadamer, in particular,
has moved from a recognition of the historicality of existence
to analyze "effective-historical consciousness"--the fusion
of the horizons of text and interpreter that occurs in historical interpretation. In the full context of historical understanding, as indicated in the conclusion to the last chapter,
it is possible to distinguish a variety of levels of meaning
or tradition: the meaning of a text in its original historical situation, the effective-historical process of tradition
in which text and interpreter are situated, the explicit application of the meaning of a text in the horizon of interpreta-

tion. This variety of meanings reflects, to a certain extent, a differentiation of the activities of the interpreter as he uses the techniques of critical history to reach the past meaning of a text, assesses this meaning in the full context of a tradition, applies the meaning in his own situation in time. Our concern now is to explore the implications of this structure of effective-historical consciousness for the interpretation of dogma.

The central presupposition underlying an approach to the hermeneutical problem of dogma through the philosophical and Protestant hermeneutical discussions is that the interpretation of dogmatic texts reflects the same basic features found in all text interpretation. The interpreter of dogma moves between the horizon of texts and the horizon of interpretation. Effective historical consciousness provides a useful schema for articulating and confronting the specific problem of the hermeneutic of dogma.

Gadamer's analysis of historical understanding involves the fusion of the horizons of text and interpreter—a dialogical relationship in which the subject matter or content of tradition emerges or "comes-to-expression." This emphasis on dialogue is important, because it preserves the hermeneutical significance both of the situation of the text and that of interpretation. Applied to interpretation of dogma, this awareness prevents a division between critical historical interpretation of dogma, on the one hand, and "faith" or "theological" interpretation on the other. It is such a severance

of methods that troubled post-Reformation Catholic theology
and which became explicit in the Modernist controversy.   The
Modernists identified the authentic meaning of the texts of
Scripture and tradition with that meaning found in their
original historical contexts and recovered in critical historical interpretation. Historical method provided a way out
of the "distortions" of the dogmatic appropriation of the
past. Blondel reacted against this objectivism by stressing
the importance of the living presence of the past in Christian
tradition, but he did so by assigning an inadequate role to
historical awareness and method. Similarly, in the classical
approaches to the interpretation of dogma, a gap was introduced between the interpretation of dogma based on faith,
authority, or the sensus fidei of the Christian community and
the work of the historian. As Walter Kasper has noted, this
severance of dogmatic and historical methods has by no means
been adequately resolved; Catholic theology is in an early
stage of the formulation of a theological method fully compatible with historical awareness.[1] One thesis of this study is
that a dichotomy of historical and theological methods is based
on an inadequate understanding of hermeneutic. By locating
the object of interpretation exclusively at the level of the
past meaning of the text, the Modernists, as Blondel observed,
overlooked the historicality and involvement of the interpreter

---

[1]Walter Kasper, Die Methoden der Dogmatik (Munich:
Kösel, 1967), esp. pp. 26ff. and 47ff.

and the hermeneutical significance of tradition. In reaction
to the Modernists, Blondel and Catholic dogmatic theology
emphasized the interpretative function of the magisterium or
of the sensus fidei of the Christian community, to the detri-
ment of critical historical interpretation. A key advantage
of the German hermeneutical discussion is that it has concerned itself with the continuity of both of these interpretative dimensions, the historicality of the text and that of
interpretation. What a recognition of this two-fold historicality means for the interpretation of dogma remains to be
considered.

I. The Situation of Dogmatic Texts

Both the philosophical and theological hermeneutical
discussions emphasize the importance of reaching the meaning
of texts in their own situation or horizon. One element of
effective-historical consciousness as Gadamer outlines it is
the sketch of the past meaning of the text. An effective-
historical fusion of horizons depends upon a distinct past
horizon or situation of meaning which is encountered by or
juxtaposed to the horizon of the interpreter. Similarly, the
Bultmannians, repeating a concern of Liberal theology, assign
a central role to critical historical method. Bultmann's
exegetical and theological studies of the New Testament demonstrate his desire to reach the original meaning of the scriptural texts as one part of the total process of existentialist

interpretation.[2] Both Ebeling and Fuchs express a similar
recognition of the importance of critical historical interpretation. As we have already seen, Ebeling emphasizes the
harmony between historical method and the Protestant principle
of <u>sola</u> <u>fide</u>. Protestantism is true to its own basic insights
when it embraces critical history and applies it freely to the
"letter" of Scripture and of tradition.

An attentiveness to the situation of the text, as Gadamer
and the Bultmannians perceive it, rests upon no new method of
history. The emergence of historical awareness and criticism
over the last few centuries has provided a variety of tools
of analysis. Philology, literary criticism, an attentiveness
to cultural and social differences and their impact on particular authors and texts--these and other techniques have
emerged in the effort to interpret historical sources. What
is the meaning of a text in its own historical situation for
author and for reader? What conscious intentions and implicit
meanings does it express? Such questions point to one dimension of effective-historical analysis, an appreciation of the
distinctive meaning of the text in its original historical
setting. The positive significance of the time-difference between interpreter and text, as we have seen, is that it makes
possible a reflective appreciation of the unique and often
quite different horizon of a historical text. The gap between
text and interpreter includes possible differences of language,

---

[2]See, e.g., Bultmann's <u>Theology of the New Testament</u>
(New York: Harper and Row, 1955).

culture, basic thought forms, and thus counters any naive attempt to identify past and present. If a fusion of horizons does finally occur, the common meaning or tradition shared by interpreter and text emerges only in the encounter of distinct and temporally separated horizons, and not in a dissolution of the gap between present and past.

The gap between the horizons of text and interpreter points to the necessity of locating the past meanings of texts. What does this principle of interpretation mean for the specific problem of the interpretation of dogma? If the focus of interpretation is upon the past meaning of dogma, then a number of possible questions can guide interpretation. Our intention here, as previously stated, is not to provide a comprehensive outline of historical method, but merely to point out some of the relevant questions that can be asked when the level of meaning sought is the meaning of a dogmatic text in its own historical situation.[3]

The basic problem facing the historian is the need to understand the language of a dogmatic text and the subject

---

[3]The following sketch of some important questions that guide historical interpretation is heavily dependent on Piet Schoonenberg's analysis of principles of interpretation in Die Interpretation des Dogmas, esp. pp. 65-69. This investigation of the original meaning of dogmatic texts is labeled "commentary" by Schoonenberg and is distinguished by him from "interpretation" in which the interpreter seeks to mediate the meaning of the text into his own horizon. For similar sketches of principles guiding the critical historical interpretation of dogma see E. Schlink, "Die Struktur der dogmatischen Aussage als oekumenisches Problem," in Kerygma und Dogma 3 (1957), 251-306, esp. 300ff., and Wolfgang Beinert, "Ewiges und Geschichtliches in der Botschaft der Kirche," Catholica 23 (1970), 361-363.

matter to which the words of the text refer, objectives which can lead to an ever wider context of interpretation. An accepted starting point in interpreting the meaning of dogma, as in interpreting other historical documents, is fixing the earliest and most authentic version of the text. In those instances where variant texts and translations exist, one form must be chosen for interpretation.[4] Beyond this formal requirement of fixing the text, the more serious problem of interpretation is a philological examination of the meaning of the dogmatic terms. What meaning did the words of a definition have in the original situation in which they were employed? The meaning of words can in fact shift as the historical context in which they are used changes. As Piet Schoonenberg has pointed out, the meaning of liber changed as the word was directed first against Pelagian and then against Jansenist positions.[5] Similar shifts in the meaning of fides

---

[4]Schoonenberg cites as an example of the need for determining the form of the text those instances when Greek and Latin versions of a council's decrees exist and the interpreter must decide on the best reading of a text in light of both. Schoonenberg, Die Interpretation des Dogmas, 66, referring to the Lateran Council of 649 (DS, 500) and the Third Council of Constantinople (DS, 552).

[5]Die Interpretation des Dogmas, 66. Part of such analysis is the determination of the literary form of dogmatic statements, e.g., the connection between dogmatic definitions concerning original sin and the aetological form of the biblical accounts of the Fall. Do the dogmatic texts qualify as more than simple extensions of the original literary forms? For further reflection on this point, see M. Lohrer, "Überlegungen zur Interpretation lehramtlicher Aussagen als Frage des ökumenischen Gesprächs," in Gott in Welt, vol. 2, (Freiburg: Herder, 1964), 521.

and haeresis have already been noted.[6] Transformations of the meaning of "person" and of "substance" have produced a gap between contemporary man and the Trinitarian and transubstantiation definitions. Such examples show the importance of fixing as closely as possible the meaning of terms in their original usage. To simply assume the accepted theological meaning of terms, as the school approach to dogma often did, or to simply take over the accepted meanings of language in one's own time, is to neglect the historical development that can in fact change the meaning of dogmatic language. The determination of the precise historical meaning of dogmatic terms is a task for careful historical analysis of the texts themselves, and not the product of the common sense presuppositions of later theology.

Investigations of the individual words employed in a definition draws the interpreter necessarily into a consideration of the "sentence" in which they occur--the dogmatic statement as a whole. What was the particular intention of a given definition? In its historical context, what was the point, the unique contribution of a dogmatic statement? This level of meaning reflects, above all, the intended meaning in the minds of those formulating a dogma. Such an intended meaning usually emerges, in the case of dogma, in response to a question or set of questions, as an effort to express the true content of faith at a particular moment in history. The question-situation prompting a definition most often comes in

---

[6]Cf. Ch. 2, footnote #35.

the form of a heretical movement, and thus the purpose of
dogma is more defensive and polemical than constructive. In
order to reach the intended meaning of the definition, it is
necessary to understand the question which prompted it--to
note the opinion that the dogma was reacting against. The
thrust of the transubstantiation statement of Trent, for
example, was not a constructive effort to state comprehen-
sively the manner of Christ's presence in the eucharistic elements. It was instead a defense of the simple reality of the
presence against a purely symbolic interpretation which the
Fathers believed to be taught by the Protestant Reformers.
The definition, as Karl Rahner has emphasized, was simply a
"logical" restatement of the biblical affirmation, "This is
my body and my blood."[7] Consequently, the question prompting
the affirmation of transubstantiation was not a need to resolve the theological disputes over the manner of the real
presence. No choice was made between the various concepts of
substance found in the theological schools of the period or
between different concepts of eucharistic change.

The text of a particular dogmatic statement alone may not
reveal its specific meaning; the interpreter may be drawn beyond the text itself to an examination of its immediate historical setting. The complete corpus of a council's decrees,
the record of conciliar debates, correspondence of the parti-
cipants and other historical sources can throw light on a

---

[7] Rahner, "The Presence of Christ in the Sacrament of the
Lord's Supper," in Theological Investigations, vol. 4 (Baltimore: Helicon, 1966), 300ff.

174

council's intention. Study of the acts of the Council of
Trent reveals, for example, that the Fathers were careful
not to identify the term transubstantiation with the opinion
of any particular theological school.[8] Subtle changes in
the wording of a definition as it passes through a process
of revision in the course of conciliar debate may point to
the specific intent of a definition as a product of a discussion and of a continuing effort to narrow the focus of the
statement. Studying the deliberations of the Fathers at
Trent, for example, Geiselmann noted that they had explicitly
rejected a formula which located the content of revelation
"partly" in Scripture and "partly" in tradition (partim/partim)
and had retained in the final decree a simple et.. This
change in wording, among other things, led to Geiselmann's
conclusion that the "two-source" theory which came to dominate
Catholic Theology was in fact a departure from the intention
of the tridentine dogma.[9]

If an adequate understanding is impossible either in
light of the dogmatic text itself or in light of its immediate

---

[8]For careful historical analysis of the Acts of the Council and of the various elements that make this avoidance of
the theological debates clear, see E. Gutwenger, "Substanz and
Akzidens in der Eucharistielehre," ZkTh 83 (1961), 258 and
E. Schillebeeckx, The Eucharist (New York: Sheed and Ward,
1968), pp. 25-86.

[9]See, above all, J. R. Geiselmann, Die Heilige Schrift
und die Tradition (Freiburg: Herder, 1962), esp. 91-107 and
277-282. A summary of a number of theologians and historians
who have supported Geiselmann's proposal is given by H. Küng
in his article "Karl Barths Lehre vom Wort Gottes als Frage
an die katholische Theologie," in J. Ratzinger and H. Fries,
eds., Einsicht und Glaube (Freiburg: Herder, 1963), p. 105,
note 25.

historical setting, a still broader horizon of investigation comes into view in order to reach the intent of a dogmatic statement. The theological, cultural, and social milieu which a particular dogma reflects can also be of importance. The theological positions characteristic of a particular era which influenced a papal or conciliar decision may, for example, need to be taken into consideration. The intent of the transubstantiation definition is clarified if the statement is read in light of Protestant eucharistic doctrine, especially the thought of those thinkers specifically named in the tridentine decrees,[10] as well as in light of the Catholic theologies of the eucharist at the time of the Council. The decrees of Vatican I can only be fully understood when located in the theological climate of the nineteenth century, and especially in the context of the thought of the Roman school, the theological outlook which had the greatest impact on the council's decrees.[11] Beyond the specifically theological milieu of a dogma, the social and cultural setting may throw light on its meaning. The development of a dogmatic tradition emphasizing the authority of the pope, for example, is inextricably tied to the long history of the political rivalry of Church and State. Yves Congar has also pointed out

---

[10]For an example of such a comparison of Trent with the thought of the Reformers see Josef Ratzinger, "Das Problem des Transsubstantiation," Theologische Quartelschrift (1967), esp. 132ff.

[11]Walter Kasper has carried out an extensive analysis of the points of contact between Vatican I and the Roman school in Die Lehre von der Tradition in der Römischen Schule.

the importance of the general concern with political and
social authority in the nineteenth century in setting the
tone of the Vatican affirmations of papal authority.[12]
Such instances show how a familiarity with the cultural,
social, and political structures of an era can elucidate
the mind-set of those formulating a dogmatic statement,
whether they were consciously aware of these influences or
not.

Beyond the immediate historical context of a dogma, a
still broader horizon for investigation is the <u>historical
tradition</u> of <u>faith</u> which has a direct impact on the formu-
lators of dogma. Dogmas are often conscious efforts either
to repeat or change earlier traditions, scriptural and dogmatic. Comparison of texts is one device for noting such a
continuity. Such a comparison reveals, for example, the use
of the word <u>homoousios</u> in the creed of Nicae, not found in
the decrees of earlier Councils, and the transformation by
the same council of Caesarea's "God from God" into "true God
from true God."[13] The development of the Christological formula through the early councils of the Church is revealed in
large part by the study of such explicit additions or altera-
tions in textual wording, and is one example which indicates

---

[12]Yves Congar has noted this interrelationship between
the emphasis on authority in the last century and the Vatican
decrees in "The Historical Development of Authority" in the
Church. "Points for Christian Reflection," in John Todd, ed.
<u>Problems of Authority</u> (Baltimore: Helicon, 1962).

[13]Cf. <u>DS</u>, 125 with 40. Cited and discussed in Schoonenberg,
<u>Die Interpretation des Dogmas</u>, p. 67.

the interpretative necessity of moving beyond the dogmatic text and its own immediate horizon in order to examine those traditional texts in whose light a specific dogma was formulated.

One focus of interpretation is the express intent of a dogmatic statement, the meaning of dogma intended by its authors. But the meaning of dogmas, like the meaning of any other historical texts, cannot be restricted to conscious intentions. Gadamer's critique of the "canon of the original reader" applies to dogma as it does to other historical sources. The meaning of texts transcends the conscious intentions of authors. The central reason for this, as we have seen, is the historicality of existence, especially exemplified in linguisticality. With his language, man is located in a horizon of which he is only partly aware in a conscious and reflective way. The concepts available in a particular language, the world view it implies, and the basic thought forms of an age affect the way in which individuals and particular cultures receive and correlate experience. Such influences are often as not prereflectively important in determining the form of a dogmatic definition. While the Fathers at Trent, for example, did not opt for any particular theological notion of substance or of eucharistic change, they did formulate the doctrine with the available theological categories of their era, namely those of Aristotelian thought. It would be naive to assume that the tridentine Fathers somehow "stepped out" of their linguistic horizon in formulating the

178

definition of transubstantiation.[14] Cultural and historical
analysis and comparison can locate the presuppositions of an
age in a way that was impossible in the historical situation
itself. The nature of such presuppositions only appear to
an interpreter approaching a dogmatic text from another historical and cultural setting. This is not to say that one
cannot grasp many elements of the horizon in which he stands,
especially as he consciously compares his own standpoint to
those of other cultures and historical epochs, or that the
interpreter ever fully duplicates the richness and depth of
the "spirit" of another age. While a reflective articulation
of one's horizon can be carried out with a certain measure
of success, however, some dimensions of the cultural particularity of an age or author may only appear to later historical interpreters. This is particularly evident in assessing
the limits and biases of any given standpoint. Such an
analysis is one dimension of interpretation directed at the
full meaning of a dogmatic text in its own horizon or situation.[15] Reaching this meaning involves interpretation directed
toward a variety of historical concerns: the language of a
text, the immediate historical setting in a council or papal

_____

[14]Schillebeeckx makes this observation in The Eucharist,
p. 56, An example of an interpreter making such a distinction between Aristotelian categories and the intention of the
Fathers is D. G. Ghysens, "Présence réele eucharistique et
transsubstantiation dans les définitions de l'Église catholique," Irénikon 32 (1959), 420-435.

[15]How far the critique of the limits of dogma may extend
--whether, for example, to contradiction--is a point to be
taken up in the next chapter.

decree, the broader social and cultural milieu, those past texts which have a direct bearing on a dogma, and the implicit presuppositions and thought forms which lie behind a given definition.

Both Gadamer and the Bultmannians point to the hermeneutical importance of reconstructing the meaning of texts in their own historical situations, a concern which applies to the interpretation of dogma as well. This critical historical interpretation of the past extends to the implicit and explicit meaning of texts in their own horizon and to the tradition process, in its past forms, in which a particular text is located. To limit the meaning of historical texts to these past meanings, however, does not do justice to the complete structure of hermeneutic. The interpreter can also ask about the point of contact between history and the present. Understanding is properly a "fusion" of the horizons of interpreter and text, and not simply a reconstruction of past horizons on their own terms. Historical understanding achieves its complete form when an encounter with history is felt, when the claim of the text asserts itself, when the truth of the text, in an effective sense, is understood and handed on. It is in the analysis of this dimension of understanding that the German hermeneutical discussion has made its greatest contribution and, we believe, has the greatest implications in the formulation of a hermeneutic of dogma. The critical historical interpretation of dogma, as of Scripture, has been a continuing concern since the nineteenth century. The distinc-

tive feature of the twentieth century hermeneutical discussion has been to integrate this dimension of historical meaning with an analysis of the historicality of interpretation,
and it is this dimension of hermeneutic, as it applies to
dogma, which now needs to be considered.

II. The Situation of the Interpreter of Dogma

Dogmatic texts have not been fully interpreted when the
historian has successfully located their meanings in their
original historical contexts, nor when he has extended the
scope of his investigation to the history of dogma in its
past forms. To reach the meaning intended by the Fathers at
Trent in the definition of transubstantiation does not automatically mediate the meaning of the dogma into the horizon
of interpretation. The primary hermeneutical responsibility
remains which is concisely described in Gadamer's notion of
the effective-historical fusion of horizons. Only when the
hermeneutical task is expanded to include the situation of the
interpreter is the structure of effective-historical awareness
complete. This is not to say that either the sketch of the
meaning of a dogma in its own historical context or the description of the history of dogma is "presuppositionless" in the
sense of nineteenth century positivism. The selection of historical data, the questions posed in the analysis of this data,
the imaginative capacity to enter the "spirit" of another age
--all reveal the impact of the subjectivity of the interpreter.
To the extent that the interest of the interpreter is in the
past as past, however, his own situation is less involved in

hermeneutic than when he explicitly raises the question of the
meaning of the past for the present. It is at this point that
the hermeneutical importance of the situation of the interpreter comes into view.

As we have already seen, the involvement of the interpreter, his awareness of the claim of the text, is one essential
element in contemporary philosophical and theological hermeneutic. Historical understanding, as Gadamer describes it, is
not complete if the attention of the interpreter is directed
exclusively to the past on its own terms. Hermeneutic instead
depends upon the location of the common tradition or subject
matter which unites past and present and which properly reveals itself or "comes to expression" in the event of interpretation. The fusion of the horizons of text and interpreter makes possible the ongoing movement of the tradition into
the future. The dialogical interaction of past and present
opens up dimensions of meaning and truth which are not available in the horizon of the text or in the horizon of interpretation taken by themselves. The path to truth characteristic
of the humanities is the ongoing anamnesis or remembrance of
the past in which historical texts speak in ever new situations of understanding. Bultmann and his successors place this
same emphasis on the involvement of the interpreter in historical understanding. Relying upon Heidegger's analysis, Bultmann
has stressed the importance of the preunderstanding of the
biblical exegete, particularly the preunderstanding of the
meaning of existence. Scripture emerges as an event in the

interpreter's experience when it is related to this preunderstanding, resolving the question of the meaning of life, and is heard as the originating power of authentic human existence. Historical interpretation of Scripture properly points toward proclamation that reasserts the claim of the text, the correlation of its subject matter with the deepest needs and concerns of contemporary man.

Following Bultmann's lead, Ebeling and Fuchs have sketched the proper preunderstanding for the interpretation of Scripture in the form of the "hermeneutical principle" brought to the text. For both men, this principle is fundamentally the questionability of existence. Like Bultmann, the New Hermeneutic theologians define preunderstanding in terms that demand no explicit faith presuppositions. "Man as conscience" (Ebeling) and "the question about ourselves" (Fuchs) are questions given with human existence which open men to a proper hearing of the Word of God. A reflective and explicit description of the gaps of meaning in reality itself and the lack of human self-identity prepare the way for the Gospel. Scripture and tradition are interpreted effectively when they are related to the problematic state of human existence in the terms appropriate to any given historical epoch. When the "subject matter" of Christian tradition is savingly reexpressed in a way that touches concrete human experience and self-understanding, then the hermeneutical responsibility of Christianity is fulfilled.

In both the philosophical and theological hermeneutical

discussions, the situation of the interpreter clearly appears as a hermeneutical problem when two objectives of interpretation are chosen. In the first place, the interpreter is drawn into the event of interpretation when he is asked to read and interpret texts in light of the subject matter or tradition they bring to expression. Interpretation in light of the subject matter identifies the tradition in which both text and interpreter are located which transcends the particular horizon of each considered in itself. The second point at which the situation of the interpreter has a clear impact on historical understanding is in the interpreter's attempt to apply the subject matter of tradition in his own situation. The reformulation of a text in one's own terms mediates tradition not as a past fact but as an existentially significant concern for men today. Interpretation in light of the subject matter and application compel the interpreter to make decisions, draw upon his personal convictions and experience, and appropriate the past in an involved, existential manner that is not so typical of the reconstruction of the meaning of a text in its own historical situation and of the past effective-historical context in which it stands. In theological terms the transition here spoken of is from explication of texts (explicatio) to the application of texts (applicatio) to present needs and concerns, from interpretation of the text to being interpreted by the text, from the traditio to the actus tradendi, from historical theology and exegesis to systematic and dogmatic theology, from text to sermon. In all of these transpositions, the interpreter is called upon to determine

not merely past historical forms of Christian faith, but to
judge what relationship past Christian traditions have to the
essential message or tradition of Christianity and to select
the proper form of Christian teaching and proclamation in the
present.

What are the implications of the historicality of the
interpreter for the hermeneutic of dogma? What is involved
in the interpretation of dogmatic texts in light of their
subject matter and in the application of dogma in the present?
Perhaps the best starting point in answering these questions
is that with which we began the analysis of the contemporary
hermeneutical discussion--a consideration of the role of
preunderstanding or prejudgments in the interpretation of
dogma. As we have already observed, Gadamer approaches the
problem of preunderstanding from a different perspective than
Heidegger, in his early writings, Bultmann, and, to a certain
extent, the post-Bultmannians. The tradition uniting text and
interpreter, which forms the interpreter's prejudgments, is
more for Gadamer than the shared existentials of world experience. Preunderstanding is not confined to an understanding
generally available in the experience of all men, open to
philosophical analysis, and neutral in regard to the claims of
faith. It is instead grounded in a concrete linguistic tradition in which both text and interpreter are located. The prejudgments of the interpreter come from his tradition and form
the point of contact with texts of the past. Gadamer provides
at this point a more adequate model for a theological hermeneu-

tic than do the Bultmannians. The linguistic tradition which
the Christian theologian reflects is that of Christian faith,
especially, although not exclusively, as mediated by the
particular Christian community to which he belongs. The prejudgments of the theologian reflect the "dogmatic" assumptions
ingrained in the living experience of the Christian community.
This is not to say that these presuppositions are beyond
correction or reformulation; the "openness" both of text and
interpreter, a point which will be more fully examined later,
counteracts any such inflexibility. The preunderstanding of
theology is not, however, necessarily "neutral" when it comes
to the content of Christian faith.

The tradition in which the interpreter stands, which
takes on hermeneutical significance in Gadamer's thought,
points to still another dimension of theological prejudgment--
the importance and validity of the ecclesial context of Christian theology. We noted in Ebeling's theology the focus on
the individual interpreter and his conscience as the final
"court of appeal" in the determination of the tradition. The
value of such an emphasis--in securing a truly critical method
and in counteracting a rigid, uncorrectable dogmatism--has
already been discussed. It seems equally clear, however, that
Ebeling has assigned an inadequate role to the hermeneutical
function of the Church as a whole. The theologian is not an
isolated and autonomous figure in the act of interpretation,
but a participant in an ongoing process of tradition which is
coterminous with a concrete historical community. The inter-

preter encounters the texts of Scripture and tradition by taking into account the tradition process which extends from them to his own period and by balancing his own interpretation against the full scope of community experience which he shares and through which he has access to the tradition. Moreover, the application of the tradition properly takes place in explicit reference to the needs and sensibilities of the Christian community. Gadamer's hermeneutic provides for this continuity of individual and community, as well as for the distinctive presuppositions and subject matter of Christian hermeneutic.

On the other hand, the Bultmannian quest for a "secular" preunderstanding in the interpretation of Christian texts, if it is not accepted as the exclusive model for hermeneutic, does have validity, particularly in two contexts of interpretation. In the first place, the critical historical interpretation of texts in their past horizons of meaning is, to a certain extent, "neutral" in regard to faith presuppositions. This judgment must be qualified because the history written by a believer is likely to differ from that written by a nonbeliever. The questions asked in the most "objective" of interpretations reflect the interests, concerns, and presuppositions of the interpreter. Consequently, the portrait of the past and those features of history chosen for emphasis will vary from historian to historian. If the historian, believer or not, is true to his method, however, the canons of evidence he employs and the verification of his claims will not be

dependent upon presuppositions unavailable to another individual who does not share his own tradition. Protestant and
Roman Catholic exegetes have drawn together in recent decades,
because they have adopted a common method of textual analysis
which is independent of their specific faith commitments.
Joint commentaries on the past meaning of biblical texts can
be written, even though disagreement may result over what
significance these past meanings have for faith today.

A second point at which a neutral or secular preunderstanding can be justly affirmed and sought is in what might
be described "fundamental" or "empirical" theology. An im-
pressive statement of the need for and form of such a method,
in relation to the problem of God, can be found in Langdon
Gilkey's Naming the Whirlwind.[16] Gilkey maintains that Christian theology in this modern period cannot simply assume the
understandability of its basic theological claims and particularly of its doctrine of God. The radical this-worldliness
of modern man and his suspicion of language describing a tran-
scendent or sacred dimension, has challenged the basic presuppositions of Christian theology. The paramount theological
need today, Gilkey maintains, is a "prolegomenon" to theology
which begins with an analysis of the universal structures of
human experience in an effort to reveal to modern man certain
dimensions of his experience and self-understanding that can
only be thematized and expressed through some form of religious

---

[16]Langdon Gilkey, Naming the Whirlwind: The Renewal of
God-Language (Indianapolis: Bobbs and Merril, 1969).

symbols, with some reference to transcendence.[17] The specific
theological task, which is distinguished from the "prolegomenon," and that aspect of Gilkey's thought of most value in
the construction of a hermeneutic of dogma, is the correlation
of the central doctrines and symbols of Christian faith with
the contemporary understanding of reality.[18] Christian doctrines can be interpreted to discover what light they throw
on significant human experiences, how they express and the-
matize the existential questions that modern man asks as well
as answers to these questions.[19] This theological work of
correlating Christian symbols and doctrines with human experience begins with the theologian's own personal insight into
the ultimate significance and meaning of a particular set of
symbols or a tradition for him. To this extent, theology begins not from the completely secular standpoint of the prolegomenon, but from a standpoint formed in the context of a
Christian faith tradition. The distinctive problem of the
hermeneutic of dogma, therefore, would occur at this latter
level of understanding, in the framework of an individual's
insight or faith experience, a position, we believe, which
agrees with the hermeneutical stance of Gadamer.

This digression into the possibility of a secular or non-
fideistic preunderstanding in the interpretation of dogma has
carried us back to the central method of theological interpre-

---

[17]The prolegomenon is presented on pp. 231-414 of
Whirlwind.

[18]Ibid. esp. pp. 415-470.

[19]Ibid.

tation and the hermeneutic of dogma which does reflect the faith presuppositions of the interpreter. The impact of such prejudgments on the hermeneutic of dogma is evident at a number of points. In the first place, the interpreter of dogma begins with the prejudgment of the importance of dogmatic texts. This prejudgment is analogous to the acceptance of a canon of scriptural writings. In both instances, the decisive introduction to the task of interpretation is a prejudgment based on the tradition in which one stands, that certain texts are particularly significant and worthy of interpretation. The dogmatic "canon" is, of course, less clearly demarcated than the canon of Scripture, and is of secondary or less normative significance. But the interpretation of dogma, like the interpretation of Scripture, begins with the understanding that certain texts have achieved "classical" importance in one's tradition and are consequently proper interpretative concerns.

Another role of prejudgments in the interpretation of dogma, more important than the simple location of texts, may also be noted. The interpreter approaches a dogma with a specific preunderstanding of the meaning of given texts. Especially in the case of definitions which have achieved a lasting importance in the community of faith, meanings are carried along with individual and community experience. The concepts of transubstantiation, of the humanity and divinity of Christ, or Original Sin, e.g., are not empty and meaningless, but are accompanied by a wealth of associations in the mind of the

interpreter. These associations, both in the form of reflective and thematized as well as prereflective and unthematized
experience, emerge from the tradition extending from dogmatic
text to interpreter and constitute his avenue to the meaning
of the text. Such prejudgments have in Gadamer's thought a
positive hermeneutical significance. They represent a legitimate reliance upon authority and tradition, and understanding
begins with a presupposition of their importance and truth
rather than, in the path of the Enlightenment, a distrust of
presuppositions as such.

A reliance on the prejudgments granted by traditions
becomes distortive only at that point when prejudgments harden
to the point that they are not open to reformulation, criticism, and possible rejection in the act of interpretation itself. "Eisegesis" results when prejudgments determine the
results of interpretation from the outset and when the interpreter proceeds without noting either the distinctiveness and
otherness of the text, or the changed situation of interpretation. One might expect that such an openness of interpretation might be particularly difficult to realize in the interpretation of dogma. The emphasis on the permanent, unchanging
meaning of dogma has in fact carried the risk of freezing the
meaning of dogmatic texts in one mold, no longer open to reformulation in light either of the renewed historical encounter
with the past or in light of the changed understanding of
reality in a given age. The corrective to such a hardening of
prejudgments lies particularly at two levels: 1) a critical

and honest process of historical interpretation of the past
meaning of dogma can point to meanings previously overlooked
or read in an incorrect light. The time-difference between
text and interpreter, as we have seen, has a positive significance because it makes possible an appreciation of the
distinctive character of the meaning of a text in its own
horizon, an awareness which can alter the presuppositions of
the interpreter. The lively discussion of the relationship
of Scripture and tradition in recent Catholic theology, for
example, emerged in large part because of a reinterpretation
of the decrees of the Council of Trent.[20] Following
Geiselmann's investigations, it was no longer self-evident
that Trent had recognized tradition as an independent expression of the apostolic witness alongside the text of Scripture.
As Geiselmann reconstructed the Fathers' intention, the tridentine decree on the relationship of Scripture and tradition
seemed instead to be much closer to the Protestant principle
of sola scriptura than was previously thought; tradition is
properly conceived as a means of interpreting and explicating
Scripture. Other similar reassessments of dogma through a
renewed process of historical interpretation could be noted--
e.g., Küng's interpretation of the Catholic doctrine of justification and his suggestion that the Catholic understanding
is completely compatible with the theology of Karl Barth.[21]

---

[20]Cf. above, ft. #9 of this chapter.

[21]Hans Küng, Justification: The Doctrine of Karl Barth
and a Catholic Reflection (New York: Nelson, 1964).

Such examples point to the importance of a continuing activity of historical interpretation of tradition. Historical judgments do in fact change, as the shifting patterns of historiography make clear. The portrait of the past, including the past of dogma, is never completed, among other reasons because the presuppositions of the interpreter and the concerns guiding historical interpretation do change from age to age, and from interpreter to interpreter. New insights into the past intentions of dogmatic texts act as a constant corrective to any given set of dogmatic presuppositions. This continuing relevance of the original intention of a dogmatic text is one element of its "normativeness." The authority of texts of dogmatic tradition rests in the continuing obligation to remember such texts in historical interpretation. They cannot properly be left behind and finally forgotten in the ongoing movement of theology and of the community of faith.

2) The second point at which the openness of the interpreter is apparent is in his awareness of the changed situation of understanding. The meaning of texts emerges as questions are posed from the standpoint of interpretation. Understanding is caught up in a dialectic of question and answer. Prejudgments are open to change because the needs, concerns, and presuppositions of what is real and important change from age to age. The questions operative today may not have been the questions operative in the original horizon of a dogmatic text. Interpretation of dogma is properly begun, therefore, not merely with the accepted prejudgments of the community of

faith, formed in its past, but with questions and presuppositions appropriate in the situation of the interpreter in a
broad sense. The quest for a neutral or secular starting
point for hermeneutic, for example, reflects prejudgments
fitting the needs of secular man at this particular point in
time. Bultmann's fruitful use of Heideggerian categories as
a preunderstanding for the interpretation of Scripture, a
technique equally possible, as Hans Jonas has demonstrated, in
the interpretation of dogma,[22] is still another instance of
interpretation open to prejudgments appropriate in the context
of understanding characteristic of the modern period. To tie
the openness of the interpreter in this way to an appreciation
of the historical particularity of the dogmatic text and to an
appreciation of the living questions of a given era is simply
to restate in the framework of a hermeneutic of dogma Gadamer's
conviction that appropriate prejudgments are worked out in the
encounter with a text. The "question" guiding interpretation
must fit both the situation of the text as well as that of
interpretation. The fusion of horizons in effective historical
consciousness thus provides the appropriate context for locating appropriate prejudgments which serve the goal of interpretation.

In the conclusion to the last chapter, we suggested that
the openness of the interpreter is paralleled in hermeneutic
by an openness of the text. This is so because of the already

---

[22]Hans Jonas, Augustin und das paulinische Freiheits-
problem (Göttingen: Vandenhoeck and Ruprecht, 1965).

mentioned possibility of new insights into the historical
meaning of texts. The historical reappropriation of dogma is
a never-ending responsibility. But the openness of texts lies
at other levels as well. Both Gadamer and the Bultmannians
have pointed out that interpretation has to do not only with
texts but with the subject matter that comes to expression in
texts. Such a transcendence of meaning, we have suggested,
lies, in particular, at two levels: 1) language carries not
only explicit intentions but a realm of meaning as well which
is only implicit or carried along with (mitgesagt) the language of the text. The full experiential reality which comes
to expression in texts may overflow the boundaries of what
can be consciously and reflectively affirmed. 2) Written language, in particular, has a certain "ideality" of meaning as
it is interpreted and applied in changing historical situations. Specific texts can be set by the interpreter in the
effective-historical process of tradition which led to their
production and which extends from them down to the situation
of interpretation. Both the implicit meanings of a text and
the effective-historical context become necessary objects of
concern in historical interpretation. The sketch of the past
meaning of texts extends beyond the intentions of an author
to the full historical reality in which authors and texts
stand. The effective-historical interpretation of texts
emerges at that point, however, when this full context of textual meaning is not only reconstructed but interpreted and
criticized to find the tradition or content which joins inter-

preter and text. The historicality of the interpreter takes
on special importance when he seeks not only the course of
history but the significance and truth of history for the
present. What do all of these observations entail for the
interpretation of dogma?

In the first place, the full meaning of a dogma transcends the explicit intentions of a particular council or
pope. A realm of meaning is carried along with the language
of dogma which extends beyond the limits of the explicitly
affirmed content of a given dogmatic statement. This characteristic of dogmatic texts is especially evident when one
looks at the experience dogmas are meant to express--the subjective act lying behind their formulation--and when one looks
at the object or subject matter with which dogmas are primarily
concerned, the mystery of God's revelation. Dogmas are properly interpreted not as formulations of abstract truths, but
as expressions of the lived experience of faith. As Karl
Rahner has noted, dogmatic statements spring from faith and
are directed to faith (ex fide ad fidem).[23] Their purpose is
not merely to speak theoretically "about" some reality--but
to communicate the reality and make it present. They are
statements "leading into" the mystery of revelation:

> If it is correct to say that the dogmatic statement,
> even where it is already real theology, is and re-
> mains a statement of faith not merely with regard
> to its object but also in the subjective act as such,
> then the dogmatic statement is determined by all the

---

[23]Karl Rahner and Karl Lehmann, Kerygma and Dogma, 88-90,
96-97.

> theological characteristics of the <u>fides qua</u>
> <u>creditur</u>.... The dogmatic statement leads
> towards the historical event of salvation, in
> spite of all its conceptual reflection. It
> renders this event present by confessing that
> it is brought about by it. It does not merely
> speak "about" this event but tries to bring
> man into a real relationship with it. And
> despite all its abstractness and theoretical,
> reflective nature, it is essentially dependent
> on the fact that this not merely theoretical
> but also existential and supernatural relation-
> ship of the whole man to the historical event
> of salvation--and not merely to some proposition
> about it--is really preserved and that the theo-
> logical statement, even in its theoretical-
> reflex character, is <u>ex</u> <u>fide</u> <u>ad</u> <u>fidem</u>.[24]

Both because dogma springs from a fullness of experience, re-
flecting the whole man and not merely the speculative intel-
lect, and because it is concerned intrinsically with a mystery
of revelation, its meaning necessarily is more than that which
can be encapsulated in a propositional affirmation.[25]

To point in this fashion to the gap between the language
of dogma and the experiential reality it expresses seems to
reassert the distinction of "form" and "content" criticized
as a hermeneutical principle in the second chapter. The expression of dogma in new terms, commonly recognized as a necessary
task of theology, implies that the content of dogma is not
bound inextricably to its original linguistic form but can be
reexpressed in new terms and categories. Such an ongoing proc-

---

[24]Rahner, "What is a Dogmatic Statement?" <u>Theological
Investigations</u>, vol. 5 (Bultimore: Helicon, 1966),50-51.

[25]For a discussion of this gap between experience and
proposition see: Simons, "Die Beduetung der Hermeneutik," 193
and Michael Schmaus, <u>Katholische Dogmatik</u>, I (Munich: Hueber,
1960), 80-82.

ess of translation implies further that the experiential
reality to which dogma refers and from which it springs is
the continuing and permanent feature of dogmatic tradition,
and not the language in which a definition is encased. The
recent controversy over the dogma of transubstantiation, for
example, reflects in part an awareness that there is a continuity in the experiential reality of the eucharistic encounter with Christ which extends from Trent to the present
day, but that this experience is inadequately expressed now,
if not threatened, by an outdated means of expression. The
search for a new theological description like "transignifica-
tion" is an effort to bring the linguistic "form" for expressing the significance of the eucharistic presence into closer
conjunction with the "content" of the dogma, the mystery of
Christ's presence as apprehended in the lived experience of
the faith community. The ambiguity with such a form-content
schema is that it carries the impression that the content of
dogma can be neatly separated from all linguistic forms.
What in fact happens in the hermeneutic of dogma is that the
reality to which dogma refers is reexpressed in another linguistic form, from another concrete situation of understanding. The "content" of dogma is never located apart from a
concrete linguistic "form." Moreover, the original meaning
of dogmas, which continues to be of significance to theology,
is only accessible through the language of the dogmatic text.
In his interpretation of the tridentine transubstantiation
decree, Edward Schillebeeckx, as we have already observed,

criticized those interpreters who have tried to separate the
intended meaning of the text from the theological conceptuality in which the Fathers thought and through which they
expressed their understanding of the eucharist.[26] The Fathers
at Trent, as all men, were located in a concrete linguistic
horizon, with certain limitations and possibilities of expression, and it is only from within that horizon that the original
meaning of the definition can be perceived. Finally, it would
be a mistake to radically separate the experience of faith
from the tensions and anachronisms that can affect the language
of faith. A crisis of language of faith can produce a crisis
of faith. While the experience of faith can sustain itself
in the absence of an adequate means of expression, a radical
gap between experience and language is neither healthy, nor,
we would maintain, can it be sustained over a long period of
time. A connection between the lived experience of faith, on
the one hand, and the linguistic means of expressing this
faith, on the other, whether it be everyday common sense means
of expression or the more reflective terms of theology, is the
necessary framework for faith and for the ongoing movement of
tradition.

The hermeneutical problem asserts itself particularly at
those points where the language of tradition, including dogma,
does not "carry" the lived experience of faith into the situation of interpretation. As Ebeling has pointed out, the
"translation" of meaning required in such instances can vary

---

[26]See footnote #14 in this chapter.

from simple philological study to an investigation of those
basic conditions which make understanding possible.[27] Similarly, the lack of understanding which produces the hermeneutical problem can extend from a gap between language and the
continuing experience of faith to a situation in which not
only the language of tradition is problematic, but the experience as well. Gilkey is right in asserting that this latter
language failure is increasingly common in the modern period
and extends even to language about God. The hermeneutical
implications of such a gap between tradition and the situation
of interpretation have already been noted. What may be required in such instances is an analysis of the basic structures
of human experience to find points of contact between traditional affirmations and the understanding of reality in a given
age. The "openness" of the text, in its reference to a realm
of lived experience never fully encapsulated in the explicit
affirmation, is here reasserted in an anthropological context.
The experiential fullness implied in Christian revelation,
which is carried along with the language of a dogmatic text,
can be interpreted in reference not only to Christian revelation and the horizon of faith but in reference to generally
shared, constitutive elements of human experience as well.

The second point at which the openness of dogmatic texts
appears is in their relationship to the effective-historical
process of tradition in which they stand. As both the outcome
and the initiation of an ongoing process of interpretation,

---

[27]WF, 318-320.

the meaning of dogma extends beyond the confines of the affirmation at the time of its formulation. The implication of this extension of meaning for the formulation of a hermeneutic of dogma points to two interpretative tasks: 1) dogma can be read in the light of the process of tradition which extends from it to the situation of interpretation. The amplification of the original meaning of a dogmatic text is not an arbitrary and extrinsic addition of content, but the effective-historical "working out" of the meaning of the text itself. A given dogmatic statement can be balanced against this fullness of tradition embodied in its own specific future as well as against the movement of tradition in a broad sense, involving even the byways and detours of theological thought, and undefined as well as defined traditional affirmations. The reference of dogma beyond a merely propositional assertion to the fullness of revelation suggests the legitimacy of assessing the place of a given dogma in the whole complex of Christian tradition. This location of dogma in the total effective-historical context of Christian faith repeats the medieval concern not to focus on individual articles of faith, but to place such propositions in the total complex of Christian truth. 2) A further dimension of the effective-historical situation of dogmatic texts is their past, and particularly their point of contact with Scripture. Dogma is properly interpreted in the light of Scripture, for it represents one aspect of the future of the biblical texts themselves. The post-biblical tradition, including dogma, constitutes the

ongoing process of the interpretation of scriptural texts.
An interpreter, consequently, can look for the continuity and
discontinuity between later phases of Christian tradition and
the origins of the tradition in the apostolic witness.
Gadamer's critical assessment of the canon of the original
reader suggests, however, that such a dependence of dogma on
Scripture will not be in the form of a simple repetition of
the original meaning of the biblical texts. As Heinrich
Schlier has noted, the interpreter of dogma who recognizes
the normativeness of Scripture is not bound to a literalistic
vision of the bible's meaning, but works in the area of experience "opened up" by Scripture; he seeks the Sache of Christian tradition itself both in light of Scripture and the
ongoing movement of tradition. His objective, for example,
is to understand God's justice not just as Paul understood it,
but rather "what it in actual fact means in the light of the
experience and reflection of the Church, which, starting
from this source, has been at work for a considerable time."[28]
Dogmas emerge at decisive points in the effective-historical
movement of tradition when the "thinking out" process culmi-
nates in judgments of important aspects of faith which then
in turn become the source for renewed reflection. "Dogma
does not signal the end of reflection, but, rather, raises
what has been thought out to an agreed level where further

---

[28]Heinrich Schlier, "Biblical and Dogmatic Theology," in
The Bible in a New Age, ed. by Ludwig Klein (New York: Sheed
and Ward, 1969), p. 123.

thought is the only worthy course of action."[29]   Interpretation of dogma in light of Scripture does not, therefore, rest
on an understanding of the "sufficiency" of Scripture which
echoes the hermeneutically questionable "canon of the original reader." The meaning of dogmatic as well as scriptural
texts is instead caught up in an ongoing process of interpretation and amplification. The perspective of one stage of
interpretation can balance the perspective of another, pointing to dimensions of the content of Christian tradition perhaps not readily perceived in a single horizon of interpretation. This broader perspective reached through the fusion of
horizons becomes particularly important in the case of dogma
for, by its very nature, dogma presents a narrow, polemically
determined perspective on the subject matter of faith. A
particular dogmatic statement is properly balanced against all
other defined dogmas as well as against important aspects of
faith which have not been formally defined. Particular dogmas
should be interpreted in light of the whole tradition of faith,
both to identify its limits and to note its distinctive contributions.

The interpretation of dogma in its effective-historical
context, including its relationship to the norm of Scripture,
can take the form of the simple reconstruction of patterns
and discontinuities in history, as earlier considered, or it
can involve a "fusion" of the horizons of text and interpreter

---

[29]Schlier, "Biblical and Dogmatic Theology," 124.

in the proper sense of the word. In this latter instance of interpretation, the hermeneutical objective is not simply an analysis of past traditions, but a decision as to the truth of tradition, an identification of the subject matter or the "tradition" within the manifold "traditions" of Christian history. A critical interpretative function is introduced which is one more indication of the involvement of the interpreter and of the impact of his subjectivity of interpretation. It is the interpreter finally who notes in the encounter with a given text the tradition uniting this text and the horizon of interpretation. Sachkritik (criticism in light of the subject matter) becomes an explicit theological concern when the interpreter seeks the effective truth of the tradition for the present.

The criticism of dogma in light of the subject matter of Christian faith carries the implication of the relativity of dogma. Dogma is a limited attempt, in a concrete historical situation, to reflectively express a particular aspect of the truth of Christian faith. The partial and relative character of dogma can be traced, in the first place, to the polemical context in which it arises. No dogma is an attempt to present a comprehensive account of the content of Christian faith. Dogma emerges, on the contrary, as a defensive effort to preserve the integrity of one dimension of Christian truth in the face of a specific threat. Only a limited presentation of the tradition of faith is intended, and this limited meaning, as already indicated, is properly balanced against and interpreted

in light of a much wider framework of Christian tradition.
Dogma is relative, secondly, because it reflects a <u>concrete</u>
<u>linguistic</u>, <u>cultural</u> <u>and</u> <u>historical</u> <u>horizon</u>, with all of the
circumscribed possibilities of experience and expression
this entails. The proper avenue to truth is finally not
through a single horizon, whether it be that of dogma or of
Scripture, but through an ever wider fusion of horizons in
which the limitations of any given horizon can, at least in
part, be overcome. This historicality of dogma is for Karl
Rahner a sign that dogma can bear the "signature of sinful
man." While it may be true, in a technical sense, dogma can
also be formulated in such a way as to block more than it
assists the perception of the truth of Christian revelation.[30]
The truth of dogma is limited, in the third place, in its
relationship to the <u>central</u> <u>meaning</u> <u>of</u> <u>Christian</u> <u>faith</u>. Some
dogmas reflect the "tradition" of faith more directly than do
others.

It is this third aspect of the relativity of dogma which
has produced in Catholic tradition a recognition that dogma,

---

[30]Rahner, "What is a Dogmatic Statement?" 45-46. Rahner
describes this limitation of dogma in this way: "One need
only ask oneself whether a statement though in itself to be
qualified as true cannot also be rash and presumptuous. Can
it not betray the historical perspective of a man in such a
way that this perspective reveals itself as an historically
guilty one? Cannot even a truth be dangerous, equivocal,
seductive, forward--can it not manoeuvre a person into a position where he must make a decision for which he is not fitted?
If such and similar questions which could be asked are not to
be rejected from the outset, then it becomes clear that even
within the truth of the Church and of dogmatically correct
statements it is absolutely possible to speak sinfully, with
a sinfulness which may be either individual, or of humanity
in general or of a particular period."

as other statements of faith, can be properly located in and
interpreted in light of a <u>hierarchy</u> <u>of</u> <u>Christian</u> <u>truth</u>.[31]
Some dogmatic statements reflect more directly the fundamen-
tal subject matter of faith than do others. One of the
ambiguities produced by a notion of the infallibility of
dogma has been a tendency to level out the importance of dogmatic statements, without regard to their specific content.
The experience of faith, however, points in another direction.
Some dogmatic definitions have been accepted as centrally
important statements of faith while others have failed to
achieve this status. It is possible, as Piet Schoonenberg
has suggested, to differentiate dogmas in light of their relationship to the foundation of Christian belief.[32] The dogmas
of infallibility or of the Assumption do not stand so close to
the central meaning of the Christian kerygma as do the definitions concerning Christ's humanity or divine sonship. In a
similar vein, Richard Boeckler has observed that something is
wrong with theology when a greater literature is produced on
mariology or the petrine office than on soteriology.[33] Beginning from the standpoint of the basic Christian kerygma, it
is possible, Schoonenberg maintains, to distinguish "central"

---

[31]An extensive historical and systematic study of the
notion of <u>Hierarchia</u> <u>Veritatum</u> may be found in Ulrich Vaneske,
<u>Hierarchia Veritatum</u> (Munich: Claudius, 1968). Cf. Schoonen-
berg, <u>Die Interpretation des Dogmas</u>, 80ff., and Richard
Boeckler, "Grenzen der Lehraussage im im römisch-katholischen
Ökumenismus," <u>KuD</u> 15 (1969), 340-353.

[32]Schoonenberg, <u>Die Interpretation des Dogmas</u>, 80ff.

[33]Boeckler, "Grenzen der Lehraussage," 346.

or "fundamental" from "peripheral" dogmatic truths.[34] The
former express in an explicit way the central affirmations
of faith which concern, above all, God in his salvific relationship to man, and thus include topics such as Christology, salvation, grace, creation, etc. The "peripheral"
dogmas take up topics of secondary importance, which stand
in a less direct relationship to the center of faith--
mariology, the Church, moral teaching, etc. The point of
such a differentiation is not an attempt to simply enumerate
those propositions most important to faith, but to show a
concern to ponder and criticize all doctrines in light of the
fundamental Christian kerygma. The theological anamnesis of
the texts of tradition is not simply a collection of the many
witnesses to Christian faith, but, as Bernhard Welte has
noted, a qualitative assessment of these in light of the one
subject matter of Christian faith. The task of theology is
to judge the continuity of phases of tradition with the central content of faith and to note as well instances of forget-
fulness and distortion.[35] Whether this reassessment can
extend to the point of contradicting a particular statement--
a position affirmed recently by Hans Küng--will be taken up
in the next chapter.

The hermeneutic of dogma, as it embraces the situation
of the interpreter and the critical reassessment of his own

---

[34]Boeckler, "Grenzen der Lehraussage," 346.

[35]Bernhard Welte, "Ein Vorschlag zur Methode der Theologie
heute," in Auf der Spur des Ewigen (Freiburg: Herder, 1965),
pp. 414-415, 419-421.

presuppositions as well as of the text in light of the subject matter or tradition of faith, reflects that concern forcefully stated by Ebeling to interpret all texts of tradition in light of the Gospel or Word of God. This hermeneutical task, we maintain, is not so uniquely Protestant as Ebeling believes, but reflects an insight of Catholicism as well. One of its implications, which has already been noted, is a need to read and criticize dogma in light of the normative expression of the Gospel, the Scriptures, with the awareness that the normativeness of Scripture is not tied to a simple repetition of its original meaning. An awareness of historicality has carried with it a recognition that the Gospel or Word of God is not simply given with the text of Scripture or dogma. The tradition or subject matter of biblical and post-biblical tradition, as Ebeling emphasizes, is not a particular complex of biblical or dogmatic truths, but the living effective power of the Word of God as it comes to expression in changing horizons of interpretation. The hermeneutical problem is to locate that interpretation which will permit scriptural or dogmatic texts to emerge in a given situation of interpretation as existentially significant statements of the salvific meaning of Christian faith. Gadamer's concern with an effective-historical mediation of tradition--one involving a fusion of horizons and application--and the Bultmannian focus on the "word-event" in which the past is mediated into the present, both point to this awareness. Dogmas are not meant to be interpreted as abstract truths, but as expressions, in

reflective language, of a reality which has salvific significance for men today. The application of dogma is finally
the communication of the truth of dogma in a way which points
to the Christian kerygma, in terms meaningful to modern man
which reach his deepest needs and concerns. The circle of
linguisticality noted in the Bultmannian movement from
scriptural text to proclamation is reasserted in a dogmatic
context; dogmatic interpretation moves from texts to an
effective expression of the meaning of the texts in the present. It is the framework of this total hermeneutical process
that the truth of dogma is discerned.

CHAPTER V

THE TRUTH OF DOGMA

I. The Truth of Interpretation

The primary purpose of this study has been to clarify
the structure of understanding involved in the interpretation of dogmatic statements. The method employed has been
to apply some of the key insights of the German hermeneutical discussion in the formulation of a hermeneutic of dogma.
If the preceding analysis has thrown light on the distinctive
"fusion of horizons" which occurs in the interpretation of
dogma, then the chief intention of this study has been
realized.

This concluding chapter is a presentation of some reflections on the truth of dogma from the standpoint of the hermeneutical problem. The topics of method and truth are not
properly separated, as the title of Gadamer's study of philosophical hermeneutic indicates. A key insight of the German
hermeneutical movement has been a recognition of the historical dimension of truth and thus of the role of tradition as
an essential dimension in man's path to truth. Man arrives
at truth by remembering the past, in an encounter with tradition. Such remembrance is properly not the repetition of the
past on its own terms, as Gadamer has stressed, but the
"fusion" of the horizons of past and present. In this new

opening and application of the past in the present, the
future of the tradition, its continuing truth and validity,
is discovered and handed on. Similarly, the hermeneutic of
dogma sketched in the last chapter pointed to the process in
which the truth of dogma emerges or comes to expression in
the interpretative movement from past through present to
future. The truth of dogma is caught up in the effective
historical movement of Christian tradition.

A question which has been raised at several points in
earlier chapters but left unanswered springs from a recognition of this historicality of truth. Is it possible to harmonize Vatican I's affirmation of a permanent or infallible
meaning of dogma with an awareness of the historicality of
dogmatic statements and of interpretation? Is not the permanent truth of dogma dissolved in the historical process of
ongoing interpretation and the multiplicity of meanings that
this tradition process includes? Is not historicism or relativism the end result of German hermeneutic? This last objection has been directed most forcefully against the German
hermeneutical discussion by the American literary critic,
Eric Hirsch.[1] Hirsch's criticism will be touched on briefly
because it points directly to some of the key issues involved
in an approach to the truth of dogma by way of the hermeneutical problem.

The problem with which Hirsch grapples is the problem of

---

[1]Eric Hirsch, Validity in Interpretation (New Haven:
Yale University Press, 1967).

the validity of interpretation. On what grounds does one
determine that one interpretation of a text is more "correct"
or "true" than another? His question is even more radically
described as the search for "absolutely valid interpretation."[2]
Two objectives guide Hirsch's search for such a method of interpretation: 1) a criticism of theories of interpretation in
the modern period, including that of Gadamer, which undermine
the validity of interpretation; 2) a constructive presentation
of some means of weighing the evidence supporting a particular
textual interpretation in an effort to determine its validity.
It is the first, critical phase of Hirsch's study which most
interests us, because it includes a lengthy critique of the
German hermeneutical discussion.

In the last four decades, Hirsch maintains, a literary
theory has developed which separates the meaning of texts from
the intentions of their authors. Such a separation of the
words of a text from the originally intended meaning prompts
Hirsch to label these views of interpretation theories of
"semantic" or "literary" autonomy. Heidegger, Gadamer,
Bultmann, and others have contributed to the notion that the
meaning of a text finally is not that meaning which it possessed in its original situation, in the mind of an author,
but that which it possesses "for us today." Such a theory
emerged in the reaction against the romanticist and positivist
"leap" into the past and neglect of the historicality of inter-

---

[2]Hirsch, Validity in Interpretation, VIII.

pretation.[3] Coupled with this new awareness of the subjectivity of the interpreter has been an emphasis on the gulf
between cultures and historical epochs which frustrates the
reconstruction of the thoughts of past figures.[4] Both of
these opinions reinforced the tendency to locate the meaning
of historical texts in the significance they possess for a
given interpreter or, in a broader sense, in a given horizon
of interpretation. With a transition from one horizon to
another or a shift in interpretative perspectives and questions, texts take on a fluidity of meaning. They can mean
different things to different interpreters. "New" meanings
emerge as texts are "applied" in new contexts and "old" meanings are left behind. Gadamer's notion of "effective-history"
involves, Hirsch believes, such a "fluidity" of textual meaning. The meaning of historical texts for Gadamer is not their
original meaning but the "effective" meaning determined from
the standpoint of interpretation. The discrediting of the
"canon of the original reader," the notion of meaning as a
product of a fusion of historical horizons, and other aspects
of Gadamer's hermeneutic locate him, Hirsch maintains, in the
"semantic autonomy" school of thought.

Hirsch's critique of such interpretative theories is
that they end finally in a historicist or relativistic attitude toward interpretative truth. The "banishment of the
author" as a norm in the determination of meaning removes

[3]Hirsch, Validity in Interpretation, 1-6.
[4]Ibid., 40.

the only real control on the validity of interpretation.[5]
To accept the theory that a text takes on "new" meanings in
each new age, when looked at from different perspectives, is
to remove at the start the possibility of objective, universally valid knowledge about the text. The openness of textual
meaning noted in earlier chapters in light of the implicit,
prereflective experience of the author and the effective-
historical context of interpretation, undermines the possibility of agreement between interpreters on what a given text
means. Depending on the individual interpreter's application
of a text or his reading of "implicit" meaning, a text can
mean many different things. It becomes impossible, Hirsch
believes, to locate a normative base for distinguishing good
from bad, valid from invalid interpretation. Gadamer's hermeneutic implies, for example, a radical indeterminacy of
meaning depending upon the particular fusion of horizons which
takes place in individual acts of interpretation. Gadamer
might say, Hirsch recognizes, that textual meaning is determinate in a single horizon of interpretation shared by different interpreters. But even in this situation, Hirsch maintains, it is impossible to say in an "absolutely valid" way
the text means this and not that. If disagreements emerge at
the same point in time as to what a text means, no method
exists for resolving the contradictions.[6] The appeal by
Gadamer to legal examples of "application" overlooks the fact

---

[5]Hirsch, Validity in Interpretation, 5, 8.

[6]Ibid., 249.

that there is in the humanities no "supreme court" for deciding the "correct" interpretation. Interpretation in harmony with the tradition is problematic because the tradition itself is not stable but in process without some recognized authority to decide what the correct interpretation of the tradition at any point really is.[7] In the domain of learning, no "papal-like" authority exists to institutionalize a given interpretation of the tradition.[8]

What the proponents of the semantic autonomy theory overlook, Hirsch believes, is the distinction between the meaning of a text in the mind of its author and the significance of this meaning as it is reinterpreted and reapplied in changing situations of interpretation. The past meaning of a text is unchanging and timeless; what an author originally intended does not change with the passage of time.[9] Verbal meaning is constant. It is not one thing "for me" and something else for another. Identifying the "verbal meaning" of a text does not mean reconstructing every component of an author's consciousness. The focus of interpretation is not on mental processes but on the object of those processes--the content intended by the author. A description of a rainbow, for example, is understandable in a later era because of the common experience, shared by author and interpreter, of the object referred to.[10] Hirsch recognizes that the subject

---

[7]Hirsch, Validity in Interpretation, 250.

[8]Ibid., 123, footnote #35.

[9]Ibid., 39.   [10]Ibid., 32.

matter intended by the author may communicate implied meanings not in his conscious awareness. The notion "tree," for
example, carries the implication of the existence of a root
system, even though the author may not have explicitly reflected upon the fact. Such unreflected upon meaning, however, must be coherent with and fit the "type" of the
intended meaning. The author, not the reader, is the normative determiner of such a typological expansion of meaning.[11]
Language may transcend the conscious intention of the author,
but it does not stand independent of his mind as an object of
analysis.[12] A past law, for example, may have demanded that
all "wheeled" vehicles must come to stop at a red light.
Years later, wheelless vehicles are invented, and the question
emerges if the law applies to them. Hirsch's response to this
question is in the affirmative, because the intention of the
original law was that all vehicles come to a stop; the "type"
includes the later invention.[13] Only by restricting meaning
in this way to a horizon determined by the author's explicit
meaning can a control be placed on interpretation:

> The explicit meanings are components in a total
> meaning which is bounded by a horizon. Of the
> manifold typical continuations within this hori-
> zon the author is not and cannot be explicitly
> conscious, not would it be a particularly signi-
> ficant task to determine just which components of
> his meaning the author was thinking of. But it
> is of the utmost importance to determine the
> horizon which defines the author's intention as
> a whole, for it is only with reference to this

---

[11]Hirsch, Validity in Interpretation, 54ff.

[12]Ibid., 23.   [13]Ibid., 126.

216

> horizon, or sense of the whole, that the inter-
> preter may distinguish those implications which
> are typical and proper components of the meaning
> from those which are not."[14]

Legitimate implications of meaning of a particular text must

fall within the intrinsic or inner horizon of the text itself,

and Hirsch suggests a number of criteria for judging truly

typological meanings: interpretation must take into account

the range of meaning in the language of a text, account for

all of the elements of a text, identify the genre of the text

(poetry, scientific, etc.), and, finally, cohere with the

author's intention.[15] This last test of valid interpretation

--careful consideration of the author's intention--is the

central factor in locating the boundaries for correct verbal

meaning of a given text.

> Now verbal meaning can be defined more particu-
> larly as a willed type which an author expresses
> by linguistic symbols and which can be understood
> by another through these symbols. It is essential
> to emphasize the concept of type since it is only
> through this concept that verbal meaning can be
> (as it is) a determinate object of consciousness
> and yet transcend (as it does) the actual con-
> tents of consciousness.[16]

Controlled, valid interpretation rests upon careful weighing

of alternate interpretations in light of legitimate typologi-

cal movements beyond the author's intended meaning.

Hirsch recognizes that the meanings of past texts may

have a different significance and application in a new horizon

of interpretation. Interpreters can move far beyond the

"type" of the text in explaining their understanding, criti-

---

[14]Hirsch, Validity in Interpretation, 221.

[15]Ibid., 236.   [16]Ibid., 47-48.

cizing the text, and/or fitting past meaning into a new situation of understanding. It is essential, however, Hirsch maintains, to separate this changing "significance" of texts from
the proper task of interpretation--the determination of the
text's "meaning." The meaning of a text does not change from
situation to situation; it is determinate, and forms the only
possible foundation for judging the validity of interpretation.
The "semantic autonomy" theory does point to the changing significance of texts through history. But if there is no fixed
meaning in terms of the text's creation, no criticism or
opinion about the text can claim permanent validity. No criterion remains for assessing interpretations of a text's
meaning or evaluating the extent to which notions of "significance" depart from the text's meaning.

> The significance of textual meaning has no founda-
> tion and no objectivity unless meaning itself is
> unchanging. To fuse meaning and significance, or
> interpretation and criticism, by the conception
> of an autonomous, living, changing meaning does
> not really free the reader from the shackles of
> historicism; it simply destroys the basis both for
> any agreement among readers and for any objective
> study whatever.[17]

The fundamental distinction between the "meaning" of a text and
its "significance" finally eliminates the possibility of valid
interpretation.

A number of aspects of Hirsch's interpretation of Gadamer
and of his concept of the hermeneutical task are open to criticism. After this criticism is developed, however, it will

---

[17]Hirsch, Validity in Interpretation, 214.

218

also be necessary to note the element of truth in Hirsch's position. In the first place, Hirsch downplays the impor-tance of Gadamer's concern to "sketch" the horizon of the text, locating its meaning in its own situation. This deter-mination of meaning is subject to the normal controls of historical argument--with an appeal to evidence, refutation of alternative ways of interpreting a given historical event or text, and so forth. The time-difference between text and interpreter acts as a "filter" for the subjective interest of the interpreter guaranteeing that his interpretation takes into account the autonomy of the text. The path of interpre-tation is not a one-sided movement from the present, with its sense of "significance," to the past. Rather, tradition in its past forms stands over the present, possibly broadening the preunderstanding of the interpreter, and opening his awareness to meanings not included in his own horizon of understanding. Gadamer would not accept Hirsch's exclusive focus on the author's conscious intention and the "type" of meaning conforming to it. The author's intention is caught up in a historical context of meaning which transcends his conscious awareness.[18] Even Hirsch is compelled to take

[18]Hirsch's concept of implicit meaning is finally more logical than historical. A movement beyond isolated texts and logical extensions of linguistic meaning becomes more important as authors are located in their historical situa-tions and as historians interpret texts as aspects of an on-going movement of historical events. Pre-reflective or non-intentional meaning becomes increasingly important in such historical investigation. For similar criticisms see Richard Palmer, Hermeneutics (Evanston: Northwestern Univer-sity Press, 1969), pp. 60-65.

account of the "implicit" meaning in a text, as his example
of the law on wheeled vehicles indicates. One can justifi-
ably ask whether the "typological" meaning employed by Hirsch
is finally more controllable than the concept of meaning
employed by Gadamer, particularly if the fusion of horizons
is accomplished in a controlled, reflectively aware manner
as Gadamer desires. The meaning of historical texts is not
whimsically or arbitrarily chosen in Gadamer's hermeneutic--
the question guiding interpretation must ultimately spring
from a recognition both of the situation of the text and of
interpretation.

Where Hirsch and Gadamer clearly part is in their respec-
tive understandings of the historicality of the interpreter.
The location of the significance of past texts and their
application in the present is not for Hirsch a dimension of
historical understanding. Nor does he assign any significant
role to the preunderstanding of the interpreter, and particularly to the existential impact of history or tradition on
the present. The autonomy of the text is preserved, but the
point of contact between its past meaning and the present is
simply not explored. Hirsch has overlooked one of two dimensions of the "truth" of historical texts and of understanding.
One dimension of the truth of interpretation is the question
whether one has understood and interpreted a text correctly,
whether he has grasped what the author of a text wanted to
say. This question of the "validity" of interpretation is
Hirsch's concern. What he neglects is a second dimension of

the truth of understanding and of texts, the truth of the
subject matter which comes to expression in texts. Hirsch
recognizes the importance of the bond between interpreter
in an understanding of the "object" discussed, e.g., the
"rainbow" or "tree." But certainly the interpreter can ask
at some point about the "truth" of the author's understanding of this subject matter. If Livy, for example, communicates a specific interpretation of the course of Roman history, is it not the task of the historian to judge this
report in light of his own critically formed opinion of the
same subject matter? This critical responsibility is even
more crucial when the "subject matter" is not a "rainbow" or
"tree" but past interpretations of the meaning of human
existence or of the meaning of the Christ-event. In the last
chapter, we suggested that the existential involvement of the
interpreter comes clearly into play in the concern with the
sachlich or material dimension of textual truth. We would
disagree with Hirsch that this aspect of interpretation can
be finally separated from the determination of textual meaning.
The interpreter's understanding of the subject matter of tradition and his interpretation of the past meaning of texts in
the tradition reciprocally interact with one another. An
understanding of past intentions of authors necessarily has
an impact on the interpreter's understanding of the subject
matter and vice versa. The full context of hermeneutic is a
movement between the original meaning of texts, the effective-
historical process of tradition in which interpreter and text

are involved, and the present horizon in which tradition is applied and handed on.

An appreciation of the importance of the critical interpretation of texts in light of the subject matter is not equivalent to accepting the Cartesian principle of universal doubt as a hermeneutical principle. The interpretation of traditional texts, and particularly of those which have assumed normative significance in a particular community, is inaugurated with a presupposition of truth rather than of error. But the location of the "true" meaning of the text is achieved only when all levels of the hermeneutical enterprise sketched in the last chapter have been completed. The true meaning is not found when the author's intention is understood and the meaning of a text located in its own horizon. What is overlooked in such a bond to the original author and reader is the historicity of truth pointed out in the German hermeneutical discussion. The "truth" of tradition is preserved only as the past meaning of traditional texts is interpreted in the full context of tradition and mediated into the present.

What Hirsch has correctly perceived is that this dialogical pattern of interpretation does carry with it the potential of a greater "fluidity" of meaning than would occur if a rigid adherence to the author's original intention were retained. This is not to say that an effective-historical approach to hermeneutic ends in complete relativism. It is not correct to say that any interpretation is as true as any other. The controlled fusion of horizons calls for a reflective attentiveness to the uniqueness of the text, to the totality of the effective-historical context, and to one's own preunderstanding. Gadamer explicitly recognizes that not every question "fits" the text, enabling its truth to come to expression. Interpretation rests on more than caprice or whim. Even with such a control over interpretation, however, an openness of meaning does occur at the level of the text and at the level of interpretation. This is so, in the first place, because interpretations of past meaning of texts can vary. Even the hypothetical possibility of "universally valid interpretation" may in fact be unachievable in a particular instance, given obscurity in the textual sources or similar interpretative problems. While a consistency in the interpretation of a given text may be reached, this is not necessarily the case. Moreover, a consistency of interpretation at one point in time does not guarantee a consistency in the future. The movement of historical study carries the possibility of the correction or even the reversal of existing interpretations. Certainly, the past meaning of some texts will be more accessible than the meaning of others. "Universally valid interpretation" must account for the latter, however, as well as the former. What universally valid interpretation means in view of this openness of historical interpretation is unclear.

A more important source of the flexibility of meaning comes with the recognition of the critical function of interpretation. When a "correct" interpretation of the past meaning of the text has been secured, the question of its truth has not as yet been settled. Criticism of the truth of a text in light of the

subject matter it expresses introduces still another openness
of meaning. An understanding of the subject matter, and an
understanding of reality in a broad sense is intrinsically involved in the horizon of the interpreter, and these enter the
process of critical interpretation. It is this historicality
of the interpreter which Hirsch tends to overlook. Differences
of opinion are possible over what the true meaning of a text
might be. The possibility of variation in interpretation in
the recovery of past textual meaning and in the critical remembrance and application of the tradition points to the hermeneutically problematic status of "universally valid interpretation"
and the location of a permanent or timeless meaning of a given
text. The implications of this judgment for a notion of the
truth of dogma need now to be more fully explored.

II. The Hermeneutical Problem and the Truth of Dogma

Hirsch's search for a permanent, irreformable meaning of
historical texts finally stands in tension with a recognition of
the historicality of text and interpretation. Such a meaning is
located, we have suggested, only by establishing too narrow a
basis for interpretation, binding it to the conscious intentions
of past authors and the logical, typological expansion of these
intentions. What is overlooked is the extent to which the
determination of the meaning of texts, and not merely of their
"significance," properly includes an awareness of the tradition
process in which both text and interpreter are located. Hirsch's
identification of "a" permanent meaning, tends to freeze the
meaning of the text at one level of tradition. The multiple

dimensions of textual meaning, at the level of author, effective-
historical process of tradition, and application or mediation
now are neglected.

Hirsch's approach to the hermeneutical problem and truth of
interpretation has been examined in detail, because it points
to a similar tension implicit in the quest for an irreformable
or infallible meaning of dogmatic texts. There is a risk here
too of overlooking the historicality of text and interpretation.
Such a danger was noted in some of the classical approaches to
dogma and tradition. The "formal-rationalist" and "mystical"
approaches to tradition both sought to guarantee the "identity"
of faith at all points in history. The unity of faith was
secured in both instances at the risk of authentic historical
awareness. Similarly, some of the traditional approaches to the
interpretation of dogma reflected a neglect of the hermeneutic
problem in the search for a permanent meaning of dogmatic texts.
The permanent, irreformable meaning of dogma has been tied to
concepts of an essential "clarity" of dogmatic texts, to the
interpretative authority of the magisterium, or to an "inner" or
"spiritual" content finally dissociated from the problems raised
by historical awareness and method. Hirsch's location of a permanent or timeless textual meaning involved a narrow focus on
the horizon of the author and deemphasis of the historicality of
interpretation. Some Catholic approaches to tradition have more
often seemed to leave interpretation confined in the present, in
the horizon of the interpreter, and, particularly, in the horizon
of the authoritative interpreter. In both instances the quest

for a timeless, universally valid meaning of tradition runs
contrary to an appreciation of the hermeneutical problem.

Hirsch's quest for a permanent meaning of historical texts,
paralleled by Identitätstheologie in Catholic tradition, tends
to "freeze" the meaning of historical texts in a particular
form. Even in quite recent Catholic notions of the "irreformable" meaning of dogma, however, the model of tradition chosen
seems to be the movement of a single unchanging "content" of
faith through a multitude of historical "forms." The task of
interpretation in such schemes seems to be the search for the
conscious intention of those formulating a dogma, with an awareness of differences of language, culture, conceptuality etc.,
and then the "translation" of this inner content into new terms.
What is sought is an a-historical core or essence of revealed
truth, propositionally expressible, which lies behind or within
the historical process of tradition. As was noted earlier, the
form-content distinction does point to an understandable concern
for the unity of faith, but it fails to do justice to the
inextricable unity of "content" and interpretation which characterizes the tradition process. The "content" of faith is
always available in particular interpretations, formed in concrete situations of understanding. The essence is never supplied purely and directly, but is always present in an interpretation determined in and directed to a particular historical
moment of the tradition of Christian faith. The full scope of
this interpretative process includes an awareness not only of
the horizon of the author, but of the tradition process as a

whole and of the problem of "application" of the effective meaning now. A full grasp of historical meaning, whether it is the meaning of Scripture or of dogma—includes an application to the changing situation of faith. Understanding is a fusion of past and present horizons and not simply a repristination of the past on its own terms. To isolate the "content" of faith from this effective-historical process of understanding is to overlook the historicality of man and of the act of understanding. The identification of the revealed truth of dogma with a single meaning or intention of a text does not do justice to the necessary unity of text and interpretation in the movement of tradition.

The belief that dogma is "irreformably" true refers less to a fixed content than to the conviction that dogmas can emerge as "effective" expressions of the subject-matter of Christian faith when interpreted within changing historical horizons. Dogmas are of normative or classical importance in the context of Catholic tradition and thus legitimate objects of a renewed interpretative concern. The permanent responsibility to "recover" dogmas by way of interpretation is, we would suggest, what the "formal" authority of dogma entails. Ebeling's critique of "Catholic" hermeneutic focuses, above all, on the formal or a priori claim to truth possessed by dogma which undermines, as Ebeling sees it, the honesty of interpretation. But is this contradiction of "formal" authority and hermeneutic necessarily the case? Ebeling himself recognizes the "normative" significance in Protestant tradition of the confessions of the sixteenth century.

> ...it is rather evident that what is constitutive
> for the existence of Protestantism is not Scrip-
> ture alone but also a certain tradition within
> the history of the Church. Alongside many tradi-
> tions which burden and distort, this is also a
> tradition which is summarized, for instance, in
> the confessional writings from the time of the
> Reformation. It would be foolish for us to dis-
> pute this point, to deny its truth, or to refuse
> to consider it as a theological problem. Protes-
> tantism would in fact sacrifice its identity if it
> sacrificed its link with this tradition of its own
> history, in other words, its link with the con-
> fessions of the sixteenth century.[19]

Moreover, Ebeling begins interpretation with a recognition of

the "normative" character of the biblical canon, fixed origi-

nally by an ecclesial decision. A criticism of the "letter" of

the Bible and of the confessions in light of historical knowl-

edge and in light of the Gospel is also affirmed, and, as an

extreme possibility, the denial of the truth of an element of a

confession or a correction of a part of Scripture or the canon.

But such a rejection, Ebeling admits, is an abstract possibility.

Existentially, it is not the way the Christian community and

interpreter recovers the tradition. Protestantism would "sacri-

fice its identity" if it gave up its link with the confessions

of the sixteenth century--rather strong language for a critic of

the Catholic understanding of the hermeneutical function of the

tradition! What Ebeling recognizes is the effective-historical

impact of tradition on the preunderstanding of the interpreter.

Protestantism, like Catholicism, is formed by the process of its

own history. It is this process of tradition, and especially

of its "classical" elements which builds the preunderstanding of

---

[19]Ebeling, The Problem of Historicity, 111-112.

the Protestant interpreter. Doctrinal authority becomes distortive for Ebeling not in the mere fact that it exists, but
when its authority is purely "formal," divorced from the question of its meaning and its "essential" (sachlich) relationship
to the Christian kerygma. The confessions and Scripture function in the Protestant community normatively, but they are
remembered authentically only when they are recovered in ever-
renewed interpretation. The authority and truth of doctrine
are finally tied to the process of interpretation which makes
them concrete--revealing doctrine to be an expression of the
essential message of Christian faith.

Is this hermeneutical approach finally so different from
the Catholic understanding? We have argued throughout this
study that it is not. An assertion of the authority and truth
of dogma finally raises without "resolving" the problem of its
interpretation. The interpretation of dogmatic texts is in
principle no different from the interpretation of any other
texts. The same obligations and difficulties confront the interpreter of dogma that confront any other historical interpreter. He must contend with the time-difference between the horizon of the text and that of the present and all that it implies
in the way of differences of language, culture, thought forms,
etc. A conviction that dogma conveys a true interpretation of
Christian revelation does not free dogma from history any more
than Scripture. Beyond this particularity of the original horizon of meaning, there is further a need to take account of the
relationship between a given dogma and the tradition process in

the broad sense, noting the interconnections between a given
dogma and its effective-historical background and future.
Finally, there is the problem of mediation or application of
tradition in the present. The historicity of revelation makes
it impossible to define the truth of dogma in a way that would
remove it from this effective-historical structure of understanding. To note the "a priori" character of an acceptance of
the authority of dogmatic tradition and to note the function of
prejudgments in the determination of meaning still stops short
of a grasp of the full hermeneutical problem. Interpretation
occurs in the "dialogical" encounter between the interpreter
with his dogmatic prejudgments, and the text itself. Prejudgments are not inflexible; they are properly exposed to criticism in the act of interpretation itself. The hermeneutical
task is not to locate an already assumed understanding of the
meaning of dogma but rather to allow the chance for a previously unrecognized aspect of its content or subject-matter
to emerge in the event of interpretation. The various dimensions of this effective-historical process of interpretation
were traced in chapter four. Interpretation reaches its goal
when, in light of the total process of tradition, dogma emerges
in a given situation of interpretation as an "effective" or
living expression of the truth of faith. Only when the focus is
kept on the effective or sachlich dimension of truth and interpretation, do the hermeneutic problem and the understanding
of truth it implies, receive their proper emphasis.

III.   The Hermeneutic of Dogma: Some Further Implications

The thrust of the hermeneutical position we have adopted is a concern to locate the "meaning" of dogma not in a single "moment" of the tradition, but in the total tradition process of Christian faith.   The identification of the revealed truth of dogma with a single meaning or intention of a text does not do justice to the necessary unity of text and interpretation.   There is an analogy between such a dehistoricization of dogma and attempts to separate individual revelatory "events" in biblical tradition from the interpretation of these events in the Old and New Testament communities.   An identification of revelation with specific historical facts or events at the origin of tradition or with a single meaning or intention of a biblical text does not do justice to the necessary unity of event and interpretation in the movement of scriptural tradition.   The difficulties encountered in the contemporary search for a clear image of the historical Jesus "behind" the kerygma as well as the difficulty in isolating the primitive or Ur-kerygma at the origin of tradition illustrates the difficulty of trying to remove a "kernel" of revealed truth from the "shell" of its historical tradition.   Investigations of Old and New Testament tradition from the standpoint of Traditionsgeschichte (the history of the transmission of traditions) have pointed to the inextricable unity of events and interpretations in Old and New Testament faith.   The similarity of Traditionsgeschichte to Gadamer's thought is apparent.   His location of the "meaning" of historical texts in the ongoing tradition-process provides a

philosophical clarification of and possible ontological foundation for the history of the transmission of traditions as it is
applied to Old and New Testaments as well as to the history of
dogma.

A. The Hermeneutical Form of Theology

Apprehension of the truth of Christian faith is inextricably bound to the remembrance of tradition. It is at the point
of the hermeneutical problem that the interests of the various
theological disciplines converge. To locate the meaning of
tradition in the ongoing tradition process is to point to the
hermeneutical concern which unites theology. The dialogical
pattern of historical understanding involves a circular movement between past and present and prevents an abstract separation of meaning "then" from meaning "now." The tension of
dogmatic or systematic method on the one hand and historical
method on the other is eased if the systematic dimension of
historical method and the historical dimension of systematic
method are kept in view. The separated methods of dogmatic and
historical theology finally come together, as Ebeling has emphasized, in a recognition of the shared hermeneutical responsibility to mediate a historical tradition.[20]

To note the final unity of theology is not to say that a
"functional specialization" in theology cannot occur.[21] The

---

[20]For Ebeling's analysis of the relationship between historical and dogmatic theology see, especially: Theology and
Proclamation (Philadelphia: Fortress, 1966), 22-31.

[21]Bernard Lonergan has presented a structure of such functional specialization in theology grounded in particular in a
distinction between historical theology directed to the past

historical task of locating past horizons of textual meaning
can be differentiated from the mediation of meaning into the
present, but only in a carefully qualified way. The questions
posed in critical history necessarily reflect the presuppositions of the interpreter, especially his life-relationship to
the subject-matter of the text. This preunderstanding is
formed in light of his community experience, understanding of
reality, cultural experience, and a number of other elements
of his horizon as well. To the extent that an interpreter
reflectively articulates his preunderstanding, he moves in the
direction of a systematic approach to interpretation and is
properly influenced by philosophy and systematic theology. An
approach to interpretation in light of such a systematic conception becomes distortive only when prejudgments are simply
read into the text and an openness to correction is lost.
Similarly, the method of the systematic or dogmatic theologian
properly presupposes and works from the constructions of past
meaning provided by the historian. This dependence of the theologian on the work of the historian is particularly important in
dogmatic theology, where the risk of sliding by historical difficulties to reach "the" true meaning of a text is a continuing
temptation. Systematic theology, as Walter Kasper has emphasized,
should think of itself as "concrete historical thought."[22]

---

and mediating theology, appropriating the work of the historical
phase of theology from the standpoint of faith and concerned
about translating the tradition into the present. See, especially
Lonergan, Method in Theology (New York: Herder and Herder, 1972).

[22]Kasper, Die Methoden der Dogmatik, 85.

Systematic and historical theology constitute two elements
within the basic hermeneutical form of theology.

B. The Problem of Infallibility

The topic of dogmatic infallibility is the subject of a
lively debate in contemporary Catholic theology. The debate
emerged particularly after publication of Hans Küng's Infallible? An Inquiry.[23] Küng's argument has a critical and a constructive side. Critically, Küng challenges the foundations
of the doctrine of infallibility, maintaining that the teaching
rests on weak historical and philosophical grounds. His constructive proposal involves a replacement of the notion of propositional infallibility with one of the indefectability of the
tradition. "Infallibility, indeceivability in this radical
sense, therefore, means a fundamental remaining of the Church in
truth, which is not annulled by individual errors."[24] Propositional statements of faith can be appropriate and even necessary,
as summaries of belief and as demarcations of truth from heresy
in those extreme situations in which the existence of the Church
is threatened. Such propositions are "binding" as a "practical

[23]Garden City, New York: Doubleday, 1971. The debate between Küng and Rahner is in English translation in Homiletic
and Pastoral Review, May, June, August-Sept., 1971. Reactions
to the book, usually critical, may be found in The Infallibility
Debate, ed. by John J. Kirvan (New York: Paulist, 1971) and in
Zum Problem Unfehlbarkeit: Antworten auf die Anfrage von
Hans Küng, ed. by Karl Rahner (Freiburg: Herder, 1971). (Quaes-
tiones Disputatae, vol. 54). See also Walter Kasper, "Zum
Diskussion um des Problem der Unfehlbarkeit," Stimmen der Zeit
181 (1971), 363-376.

[24]Küng, Infallibility?, 181.

234

ruling on terminology"--as a guide to the appropriate language of faith in a given historical situation. Such a ruling is not, however, binding for eternity.[25] It, like any other doctrinal statement, is subject to reversal in the future. A recognition of the binding character of propositions does not mean having to accept their infallibility.[26] Many complex questions are involved in Küng's study, and a complete consideration of them would take us beyond the limits of this work. Instead, one aspect of the infallibility problem will be noted--its point of contact with the hermeneutical problem. Both in Küng's book and in the work of his critics there is a lack of a discussion of the hermeneutical problem.[27] Without claiming to settle the issue of infallibility, which is in an early stage of debate, I would like to note some connections between the hermeneutic of dogma outlined in his study and the concept of infallibility.

In the first place, a recognition of infallibility, as noted before, points to but does not resolve the hermeneutical problem. To say that the meaning of dogma, when properly understood, is a true interpretation of Christian revelation which cannot be contradicted, does not settle the question of what that meaning might be. The meaning of dogma, when the problem of historicality is taken seriously, emerges in the effective-

---

[25]Küng, _Infallibility_?, 148.

[26]_Ibid._, 151.

[27]Luigi Sartori's article on Küng's hermeneutical principles touches on the hermeneutical problem in an unsatisfactory way. "Uberlegungen zu den hermeneutischen Kriterien von H. Küng," in _Zum Problem Unfehlbarkeit_, 71-96.

historical process of interpretation outlined earlier. Dogmatic texts are properly interpreted not in isolation from tradition as a whole, but when located in the total complex of
community experience. The situation of the text, cultural and
historical background, the place of a particular definition in
the framework of other dogmas and undefined traditions, interpretation of dogma in light of Scripture, an attentiveness to
the needs and questions in the horizon of interpretation--these
and other elements enter interpretation. We have emphasized
that one aspect of meaning cannot be torn from the tradition-
process and identified a priori as "the" meaning of the text.
Interpretation always occurs in a concrete situation, from a
particular horizon of understanding, and, with this historicality, a "flexibility" of meaning is introduced. One of the
ambiguities in Küng's Infallible? is that he has defined infallibility in terms of infallible propositions, clear and distinct
ideas, and thus has employed an unhistorical concept of dogmatic
meaning.[28] It is not surprising that a number of Küng's critics
have found a gap between his definition of dogma and that which
guides the contemporary Catholic theological discussion, which
is more attuned to the problem of historicality than was the
theology of the schools.

To approach the interpretation of dogma from the standpoint
of its meaning rather than its formal claim to authority or truth
points to still other implications. Dogma is properly "true"

_____
[28]Cf. Kasper, "Zum Diskussion um des Problem der Unfehlbarkeit," 371. Kasper notes that Vatican I did not speak of infallible propositions or formulations, but of infallible "meaning."

not in a merely formal but in a material sense. A concern
with the hermeneutical problem brings into focus the pragmatic
or effective dimension of truth. Dogma is true to the extent
that it touches experience, opening up perspectives on reality
and self, pointing to existentially significant meanings in
Christian self-understanding. A concern to ground the truth of
dogma in material rather than juridical considerations emerged
earlier in the sketch of the interpretation of dogma in light
of its subject matter or content. Setting dogma in the context
of the scriptural witness, an identification of a hierarchy of
dogmatic truths, the necessary criticism of the limitations
imposed on dogmatic formulations by their situations--these and
other aspects of historicality have been discussed. A related
topic is the need to set dogma in the context of the faith of
the Church as a whole. Vatican I recognized the bond between
papal infallibility and the faith of the Christian community
without spelling out the precise interrelationship.[29] A pope
or Council is not infallible in an autonomous manner, but as an
expression or reflection of the community sense of faith. The
responsibility for the Pope to consult the Church in any act of
dogmatic definition is one conclusion which has emerged from an

---

[29]The infallibility of the Church as a whole was taken up
in chapters VIII and IX of the first draft of the Constitution
on the Church. See Neuner-Roos, The Teaching of the Catholic
Church, ed. by Karl Rahner (New York: Herder, 1967), nos. 366-
367, pp. 217-218. This link between the infallibility of the
whole Church and councils and papacy has become a central theme
in modern theological treatments of infallibility. See, e.g.,
Rahner-Lehmann, Kerygma and Dogma, 36. For an analysis of the
debates at Vatican I on the subject see Gustave Thils, L'Infail-
libilité Pontificale: Source-Conditions-Limites (Gembloux,
1969), and Walter Kasper, "Primat und Episkopat nach dem Vati-
kanum I," in Glaube und Geschichte (Mainz, 1970), 415-441.

appreciation of the ecclesial foundation of infallibility.
Still other developments of Vatican I's teaching have also been
suggested. Walter Kasper, for example, has noted that the precise conditions under which a Pope teaches infallibly were not
adequately defined by Vatican I.[30] Starting from this lack of
clear teaching on the subject and from an appreciation of the
faith of the Church, he has suggested that purely formal criteria of infallibility--a solemn statement on matters of faith
and morals, etc.--may be insufficient as a test of those statements which are infallible. The question is open, Kasper maintains, whether the pope speaks infallibly whenever such conditions are met or only when he in fact reflects the faith of the
Church.[31] To speak of a priori infallible teaching, as both
Küng and Ebeling do, is inaccurate. There is an a posteriori
dimension to infallible teaching, grounded in the correlation
which must exist between such teaching, the revealed truth of
faith, and the faith of the Church as a whole. This origin of
dogmas in the faith of the Church points also to the concern of
interpretation: "What applies to the definitions of dogmas
applies also to their interpretation: they are true and binding
not as isolated a priori clear and error-free propositions, but
they are true and binding in the way in which they are understood in the ecclesial community."[32] The truth of dogma is veri-

[30]Kasper, "Zum Diskussion um des Problem der Unfehlbarkeit,"
368.

[31]Ibid.

[32]Ibid., 372.

fied by its point of contact with the faith of the Church.

To the agreement between a dogma and the faith of the
community at the time of a definition, another level of agreement might be noted--the subsequent process of the reception
of dogma in the Church. This process of reception is very
little treated in Catholic theology, largely because of the
teaching of Vatican I that the authority of dogma does not depend on the consent of the Church.[33] To deny another level of
"legal" authority, which is what Vatican I had in mind, says
nothing about the effective or existential impact of a definition as an important aspect of its meaning and truth. In an
article on Lonergan's use of Scripture as a source in theology,
Quentin Quesnell has characterized this effective history of
dogma as an interpretative principle in a particularly clear
and striking way. The presupposition of the theologian and
community in interpreting dogma is that dogmas are true. But
if they are true they must correlate with the understanding of
reality and truth reflected in Christian faith experience in any
given age. "Hence of any alternative possibilities for interpreting a dogma, you always choose the most intelligible, the
most reasonable, the one which most promotes the advance of man
towards God (to the best of your understanding)."[34] This same

---

[33]The lack of a theological discussion of the reception of
dogma has been noted by Karl Lehmann, "Die dogmatische Denkform
als hermeneutisches Problem," Evangelische Theologie 30 (1970),
484. An exception is A. Grillmeier, "The Reception of Church
Councils," Foundations of Theology, ed. by Philip McShane, S.J.
(Notre Dame: Notre Dame University Press, 1972), pp. 102-114.

[34]"Theological Method on the Scripture as Source," in
Foundations of Theology, 184, cf. 189-190 and ft. #54, pp. 250 ff.

correlation of an understanding of what is real and true with
the meaning of dogma occurs in the history of the Church's
reception of a dogmatic definition. The interpretation of dogma becomes especially crucial when definitions seem to contradict the experience of a later community. In such instances,
the community draws the conclusion that nothing was defined, or
that the meaning of the definition has not been correctly under-
stood--in other words the dogma is interpreted in the "best
possible way" and brought into harmony with the experience of
the community.[35] There is an insufficient development in
Quesnell's scheme of the possibility of a correction of the
community's sense of reality and truth by the tradition. His
basic purpose is, however, justified; the effective-historical
process of the interpretation of dogma, as it is verified in
the act of faith of the community, is an essential dimension in
the determination of its meaning and effective truth.

Accepting the possibility of a perception in the Christian
community that a dogma seems to stand in contradiction with
experience, the normal inclination, as Quesnell points out, is
to interpret the tradition in the best possible way. Flat rejection of a normative teaching as false, which Küng supports
in extreme cases, is not the normal course of action in the reception and interpretation of texts of classical importance.
This is especially true in the case of those texts which reflect
the central content of faith and which have assumed places of
great significance in the life of the Church. A questioning of

[35]Quesnell, "Theological Method," 184, 189-190, ft. #54,
250ff.

the meaning of the christological definitions of the early
Christian era should cause more uneasiness and a more urgent
search for a way of interpretation than a crisis of meaning
in mariological beliefs or in the teaching on papal infallibility. Some dogmas, in fact, hold higher positions in the
hierarchy of truth than do others. If the sachlich and effective context of infallibility is kept in mind, might it not be
possible to accept the possibility of a contradiction of propositions, on the periphery of faith, originally proposed as
formal dogmas? This would be a possibility especially in the
case of those dogmas which have not in fact assumed places of
importance in the life experience of the community. As such
statements are called in question, we would suggest, what may
be involved is the growth of an awareness that some teachings
thought to be infallible expressions of the central and lasting
meaning of Christian faith were in fact, a posteriori, not in
this class of affirmations at all. A careful process of interpretation throughout the theological community as a whole, and
in light of all the dimensions of meaning suggested in chapters
three and four, would precede such a judgment of error. The
final test would be the reception of such a judgment by the
Church. A recognition of the finite character of all judgments
of meaning and truth, granted the concrete historical situation
of all interpretation, would further suggest, however, that
such a judgement of error in a particular situation might be
reversed by a later generation. A "universally valid" judgment
of error is as questionable as a "universally valid" judgment

of truth. It is for this reason that it is not in order to
carry out a revision of the canon of Scripture, for example,
simply because a given generation has difficulty in finding the
meaning in a part of the canonical writings. A material rather
than a formal understanding of infallibility is needed. Infallible statements of faith emerge when the community commits itself to a decision which in fact reflects the central content
of Christian faith and which is necessary when the very existence of the Church and the "cause" (Sache) of Christ is threatened. To deny such affirmations would be to deny the meaning of
Christian faith in a fundamental way.[36] The meaning of such
texts emerges for the interpreter in the hermeneutical process
outlined in chapter four, as they are interpreted in their own
historical context, in light of the effective-historical process
of tradition, and mediated into the horizon of interpretation.

Whatever decision is taken on the hypothetical possibility
of a contradiction of particular dogmatic statements, this is,
we would emphasize again, a question of secondary importance.
The key issue in the modern era is not the formal truth of dogma or the formal possibility of contradiction, but the question
what dogmas mean and their effective truth. The hermeneutical
problem emerges in the awareness that dogma is today more often
a hindrance than an aid to faith. Perhaps some of this difficulty is a product of an inadequate discussion of the structure
of understanding involved in the interpretation of dogmatic

---

[36]For a similar position on infallibility see Schoonenberg,
Die Interpretation des Dogmas, 81-82.

statements. If an approach to the hermeneutical problem of dogma through the German hermeneutical discussion has furthered this discussion, then the purpose of this study has been realized.

BIBLIOGRAPHY

Beinert, Wolfgang. "Ewiges und Geschichtliches in der Botschaft der Kirche." Catholica, 23 (1970), 345-368.

Berkouwer, G. C. The Second Vatican Council and the New Catholicism. Grand Rapids: Eerdmans, 1965.

Beumer, Johannes. "'Res fidei et morum': Die Entwicklung
eines theologischen Begriffs in den Dekreten der drei
letzten Ökumenischen Konzilien." Annuarium Historiae Conciliorum, 2 (1970), 112-134.

_____. Theologie als Glaubensverständnis. Würzburg:
Echter, 1953.

Bévenot, Maurice. "Faith and Morals in the Council of Trent and
Vatican I." Heythrop Journal, 3 (1962), 15-30.

Blondel, Maurice. History and Dogma. New York: Holt, Rinehart,
and Winston, 1964.

Boeckler, Richard. "Grenzen der Lehraussage im römisch-katholischen Ökumenismus." Kerygma und Dogma, 15 (1969),
340-353.

_____. Der moderne römisch-katholische Traditionsbegriff.
Göttingen: Vandenhoeck & Ruprecht, 1967.

Brown, Raymond. "The Problems of the 'Sensus Plenior,'"
Ephemerides Theologicae Lovanienses, 43 (1967), 460-469.

_____. The Sensus Plenior of Sacred Scripture. Baltimore:
St. Mary's Press, 1955.

Bulst, Werner. Revelation. New York: Herder and Herder, 1965.

Bultmann, Rudolf. History and Eschatology. New York: Harper
and Row, 1957.

_____. "Introduction: Viewpoint and Method." Jesus and
the Word. New York: Scribners, 1958.

_____. "Is Exegesis without Presuppositions Possible,"
Existence and Faith. Cleveland: World Publishing Co.,
1963.

Bultmann, Rudolf. "The Problem of Hermeneutics." Essays: Philosophical and Theological. London: SCM Press, 1955.

_____. Theology of the New Testament. 2 vols. New York: Harper and Row, 1955.

Chadwick, O. From Bossuet to Newman. The Idea of Doctrinal Development. Cambridge: Cambridge University Press, 1957.

Congar, Yves. "The Historical Development of Authority in the Church. Points for Christian Reflection." Problems of Authority. ed. by John Todd. Baltimore: Helicon, 1962.

_____. The History of Theology. Garden City: Doubleday, 1968.

_____. Tradition and Traditions in the Church. New York: Macmillan, 1966.

Conzelmann, Hans. "Zur Analyse der Bekenntnisformel I. Kor. 15:3-5." Evangelische Theologie, 25 (1965), 1-15.

Coreth, Emerich. Grundfragen der Hermeneutik. Freiburg: Herder, 1969.

David, J. "Glaube und Sitten: eine missverständliche Formel." Orientierung, 35 (1971), 32-34.

Deneffe, A. "Dogma. Wort und Begriff." Scholastik, 6 (1931), 384-400; 505-538.

Dilthey, Wilhelm. The Essence of Philosophy. Chapel Hill: University of North Carolina Press, 1961.

_____. Pattern and Meaning in History. New York: Harper and Row, 1961.

_____. "The Understanding of Other People and their Life Expressions." Theories of History. ed. by Patrick Gardiner. Glencoe: Free Press, 1959.

Duss-von-Werdt, J. Theologie als Glaubenserfahrung: eine Skizze zur Grundlegung der Theologischen Hermeneutik und Topik. Einsiedeln: Bonziger, 1969.

Ebeling, Gerhard. "Hermeneutik." Die Religion in Geschichte und Gegenwart. 3rd edition., III.

_____. The Problem of Historicity in the Church and Its Proclamation. Philadelphia: Fortress Press, 1967.

_____. Theology and Proclamation: Dialogue with Bultmann. Philadelphia: Fortress Press, 1966.

Ebeling, Gerhard. "Tradition: Dogmatisch." Die Religion in Geschichte und Gegenwart. 3rd edition., VI.

_____. Word and Faith. Philadelphia: Fortress Press, 1963.

_____. The Word of God and Tradition. Philadelphia: Fortress Press, 1968.

_____. Wort und Glaube. Bd. II. Tübingen: J. C. B. Mohr, 1969.

Feiner, Johannes and Löhrer, Magnus, eds. Mysterium Salutis, I. Einsiedeln: Benziger, 1965.

Finkenzeller, Josef. "Überlegungen zur Sprachgestalt und zur Grenze des Dogmas." Münchener Theologische Zeitschrift, 21 (1970), 216-236.

Fransen, Piet. "The Authority of Councils." Problems of Authority. ed. by John Todd. Baltimore: Helicon, 1962.

_____. "Réflexions sur l'anathème au concile de Trente." Ephemerides Theologicae Lovanienses, 29 (1953), 657-672.

Fuchs, Ernst. Hermeneutik. 3rd ed. Stuttgart: R. Müllerschon Verlag, 1963.

_____. Marburger Hermeneutik. Tübingen: J. C. B. Mohr, 1968.

Gadamer, Hans Georg. Kleine Schriften, I. Philosophie-Hermeneutik. Tübingen: J. C. B. Mohr, 1967.

_____. "Tradition: I. Phänomenologisch." Die Religion in Geschichte und Gegenwart. 3rd edition, VI.

_____. "Verstehen." Die Religion in Geschichte und Gegenwart. 3rd edition, VI.

_____. Wahrheit und Methode. Grundzüge einer philosophischen Hermeneutik. Tübingen: J. C. B. Mohr, 1965.

Garrigou-Lagrange, R. "L'immutabilité des vérités définies et le surnaturel." Angelicum, XXV (1948), 285-298.

_____. "L'immutabilité du dogme selon le concile du Vatican et le relativisme." Angelicum, XXVI (1949), 309-322.

Geiselmann, J. R. "Dogma." Handbuch Theologischer Grundbegriffe, I. Munich: Kösel, 1962.

_____. Die Heilige Schrift und die Tradition. Freiburg: Herder, 1962.

Geiselmann, J. R. <u>Die katholische Tübinger Schule</u>. Freiburg: Herder, 1964.

Geisser, Hans. "Hermeneutische Probleme in der neueren römisch-katholischen Theologie." <u>Erneuerung der Einen Kirche. Festschrift für Heinrich Bornkamm</u>. Göttingen: Vandenhoeck & Ruprecht, 1966.

Ghysens, D. G. "Présence réele eucharistique et transsubstantiation dans les définitions de l' Eglise catholique." <u>Irénikon</u>, 32 (1959), 420-435.

Gilkey, Langdon. <u>Naming the Whirlwind: The Renewal of God-Language</u>. Indianapolis: Bobbs & Merril, 1969.

Gloege, G. "Dogma." <u>Die Religion in Geschichte und Gegenwart</u>. 3rd edition, II.

Grillmeier, A. "The Reception of Church Councils." <u>Foundations of Theology</u>. ed. by Philip McShane. Notre Dame: University of Notre Dame Press, 1971.

Gutwenger, E. "Substanz und Akzidens in der Eucharistielehre." <u>Zeitschrift für katholische Theologie</u>, 83 (1961), 257-294.

Habermas, Jürgen. "Zur Logik der Sozialwissenschaft." <u>Philosophische Rundschau</u>, Beiheft 5, Kap. III. Tübingen: J. C. B. Mohr, 1967.

Hammans, H. <u>Die neueren katholischen Erklärungen der Dogmenentwicklung</u>. Essen: Ludgerus Verlag, 1965.

Heidegger, Martin. <u>Being and Time</u>. New York: Harper and Row, 1962.

Hirsch, Eric. <u>Validity in Interpretation</u>. New Haven: Yale University Press, 1967.

Hödl, L. "Articulus Fidei." <u>Einsicht und Glaube. Festschrift für G. Söhngen</u>. ed. by G. Söhngen. Freiburg: Herder, 1962.

Jonas, Hans. <u>Augustin und des paulinische Freiheitsproblem</u>. Göttingen: Vandenhoeck & Ruprecht, 1965.

Kasper, Walter. <u>Dogma unter dem Wort Gottes</u>. Mainz: Grünewald, 1965.

_____. "Geschichtlichkeit der Dogmen?" <u>Stimmen der Zeit</u>, 179 (June, 1967), 401-416.

_____. <u>Glaube und Geschichte</u>. Mainz: Grünewald, 1970.

_____. <u>Die Lehre von der Tradition in der Römischen Schule</u>. Freiburg: Herder, 1962.

Kasper, Walter. _Die Methoden der Dogmatik_. Munich: Kösel, 1966.

_____. "Zum Diskussion um des Problem der Unfehlbarkeit." _Stimmen der Zeit_, 181 (1971), 363-376.

Keller, Albert. "Hermeneutik und christlicher Glaube." _Theologie und Philosophie_, 44 (1969), 25-42.

Kimmerle, H. "Hermeneutical Theory or Ontological Hermeneutic." _History and Hermeneutic_. ed. by Robert Funk. Journal for Theology and Church, IV. New York: Harper and Row, 1967.

Kirven, John J., ed. _The Infallibility Debate._ New York: Paulist, 1971.

Kösters, Reinhard. "Dogma und Bekenntnis bei Gerhard Ebeling." _Catholica_, 24 (1970), 51-66.

Krüger, Gerhard. _Freiheit und Weltverwaltung_. Freiburg-Munich: Karl Alber, 1958.

Kümmerlinger, Hans. "Es ist Sache der Kirche, 'iudicare de vero sensu et interpretatione scriptuarum sanctarum!'" _Theologische Quartelschrift_, 149 (1969), 282-296.

Küng, Hans. _Infallibility? An Inquiry_. New York: Doubleday, 1971.

_____. _Justification: The Doctrine of Karl Barth and a Catholic Reflection_. New York: Nelson, 1964.

_____. _Structures of the Church_. Notre Dame: University of Notre Dame Press, 1964.

Lakner, F. "Zur Frage der Definibilität einer geoffenbarten Wahrheit." _Zeitschrift für Katholische Theologie_, 85 (1963), 322-338.

Lang, Albert. "Der Bedeutungswandel der Begriffe 'fides' und 'haeresis' und die dogmatische Wertung der Konzilentscheidungen von Vienne und Trient." _Münchener Theologische Zeitschrift_, 4 (1953), 133-146.

_____. _Die theologische Prinzipienlehre der mittelalterlichen Scholastik_. Freiburg: Herder, 1964.

Lapointe, R. _Les trois dimensions de l'herméneutique_. Paris: J. Gabalda, 1967.

Latourelle, Réné. _Theology of Revelation_. New York: Alba, 1966.

248

Lehmann, Karl. "Die dogmatische Denkform als hermeneutisches Problem." Evangelische Theologie, 30 (1970), 469-487.

_____. "Hermeneutik." Sacramentum Mundi, II.

Lengsfeld, Peter. Überlieferung und Schrift in der evangelischen und katholischen Theologie der Gegenwart. Paderborn: Bonifacius, 1960.

Löhrer, Magnus, O.S.B. "Überlegungen zur Interpretation lehramtlicher Aussagen als Frage des ökumenischen Gesprächs." Gott in Welt, II. Freiburg: Herder, 1964, 499-523.

Lonergan, Bernard. Doctrinal Pluralism. Milwaukee: Marquette University Press, 1971.

_____. Method in Theology. New York: Herder, 1972.

_____. "Theology in its New Context." Theology of Renewal, I. ed. by L. K. Shook. New York: Herder, 1968.

Loretz, Oswald and Strolz, W., eds. Die hermeneutische Frage in der Theologie. Freiburg: Herder, 1968.

Marlé, R. Au coeur de la crise moderniste. Le dossier inédit d'une controverse. Paris: Montaigne, 1960.

_____. Introduction to Hermeneutics. New York: Herder, 1967.

Moran, Gabriel. Theology of Revelation. New York: Herder, 1966.

Mussner, F. "'Evangelium' und 'Mitte' des Evangeliums." Gott im Welt, I. Freiburg: Herder, 1964, 492-514.

Neuenzeit, P. et al. Die Funktion der Theologie in Kirche und Gesellschaft. Beiträge zu einer notwendiges Diskussion. Munich, 1969.

Palmer, Richard. Hermeneutics. Evanston: Northwestern University Press, 1969.

Pinard, H. "Dogme." Dictionnaire d'archéologie chrétienne et de liturgie, I. Paris, 1924ff.

Pottmeyer, Hermann J. "Kirchliche Lehrautorität und Wissenschaft ein Gegensatz?" Münchener Theologische Zeitschrift, 20 (1969), 85-103.

Quesnell, Quentin. "Theological Method on the Scripture as Source." Foundations of Theology. ed. by Philip McShane. Notre Dame: University of Notre Dame Press, 1971, 162-193.

Rahner, Karl. "Considerations on the Development of Dogma." Theological Investigations, IV. Baltimore: Helicon, 1966.

_____. "The Development of Dogma." Theological Investigations, I. Baltimore: Helicon, 1961.

_____ and Pozo, Candido. "Dogma." Sacramentum Mundi, II.

_____. "The Historical Dimension in Theology." Theology Digest. Sesquicentennial Issue. Feb. 1968. School of Divinity, St. Louis University, 1968, 30-43.

_____ and Lehmann, Karl. Kerygma and Dogma. New York: Herder, 1969.

_____. "The Presence of Christ in the Sacrament of the Lord's Supper." Theological Investigations, IV, Baltimore: Helicon, 1966.

_____ and Ratzinger, Joseph. Revelation and Tradition. New York: Herder and Herder, 1966.

_____. "What is a Dogmatic Statement?" Theologidal Investigations, V. Baltimore: Helicon, 1966.

_____, ed. Zum Problem Unfehlbarkeit: Antworten auf die Anfrage von Hans Küng. Freiburg: Herder, 1971.

Ranft, J. "Dogma: I (semasiologisch)." Reallexikon für Antike und Christentum, IV.

Ratzinger, Josef. Das Problem der Dogmengeschichte in der Sicht der katholischen Theologie. Cologne: Opladen, 1966.

Robinson, James M. "Introduction." The New Hermeneutic. New Frontiers in Theology, II. New York: Harper and Row, 1964.

Scheffczyk, L. "Die Auslegung der Heiligen Schrift als dogmatische Aufgabe." Münchener Theologische Zeitschrift, 15 (1963), 190-204.

Schillebeeckx, E. The Eucharist. New York: Sheed and Ward, 1968.

_____. Revelation and Theology, I. New York: Sheed and Ward, 1967.

_____. "Towards a Catholic Use of Hermeneutics." God the Future of Man. New York: Sheed and Ward, 1968, 1-51.

Schleiermacher, Friedrich. Hermeneutik. ed. by H. Kimmerle. Heidelberg: C. Winter, 1959.

250

Schlette, H. R. "Dogmengeschichte und Geschichtlichkeit des
     Dogmas." _Münchener Theologische Zeitschrift_, 14 (1963),
     243-252.

Schlier, Heinrich. "Biblical and Dogmatic Theology." _The
     Bible in a New Age_, ed. by Ludwig Klein. London-N. Y.:
     Sheed and Ward, 1969, 112-132.

_____. "Kerygma und Sophia. Zur neutestamentlichen
     Grundlegung der Dogma." _Die Zeit der Kirche_. Freiburg:
     Herder, 1957.

Schlink, E. "Die Struktur der dogmatischen Aussage als ökumeni-
     schen Problem." _Kerygma und Dogma_, 3 (1957), 251-306.

Schmaus, Michael. _Dogma_, I. New York: Sheed and Ward, 1968.

_____. _Katholische Dogmatik_, I. Munich: Hueber, 1960.

_____. _Preaching as the Sacrament of the Encounter with
     God_. Staten Island: Alba House, 1966.

Schnackenburg, Rudolf. "Zur Auslegung der Schrift in unserer
     Zeit." _Bibel und Leben_, 4 (1964), 220-236.

Schoonenberg, P. J. ed. _Interpretation des Dogmas_. Düssel-
     dorf: Patmos, 1969.

Schüller, B. "Bemerkungen zur authentischen Verkündigung des
     kirchlichen Lehramtes." _Theologie und Philosophie_, 42
     (1967), 534-551.

Seckler, Max. "Die Theologie als kirchliche Wissenschaft nach
     Pius XII und Paul VI." _Theologische Quartelschrift_, 149
     (1969), 209-235.

Simons, Eberhard. "Die Bedeutung der Hermeneutik für die katho-
     lische Theologie." _Catholica_, 21 (1967), 184-213.

_____. and Hecker, Konrad. "Philosophische Prolegomena zu
     einer theologischen Hermeneutik." _Catholica_, 23 (1969),
     62-82.

_____. and Hecker, Konrad. _Theologisches Verstehen_. Düssel-
     dorf: Patmos, 1969.

Stachel, Günter. _Die neue Hermeneutik: Ein Überblick_. Munich:
     Kösel, 1967.

Valeske, Ulrich. _Hierarchia Veritatum_. Munich: Claudius, 1968.

Welte, Bernhard. _Auf der Spur des Ewigen_. Freiburg: Herder,
     1965.

DATE DUE